"This is a book for everybody. It doesn't matter who you are or where you are. I promise you, if you will allow the principles set forth here to sink in, you will be a different person. I have yet to see a person who has learned how to be a Loved Person continue to live in defeat."

Marie Chapian believes that a gut-level grasp of God's love will dramatically change anyone's life. She's seen it happen to others. She's felt it in her own life. And she's anxious to help you experience it yourself. It all begins with a simple but profound truth: You are a "Loved Person."

Read on.

BY Marie Chapian

Help Me Remember . . . Help Me Forget
  (formerly *The Emancipation of Robert Sadler*)
Of Whom the World Was Not Worthy
Free to Be Thin
In the Morning of My Life
  (the story of singer Tom Netherton)
Telling Yourself the Truth
  (with Dr. William Backus)
Escape From Rage
Fun to Be Fit
Love and Be Loved

TO LOVE AND BE LOVED

Marie Chapian

Power Books

Fleming H. Revell Company
Old Tappan, New Jersey

Library of Congress Cataloging in Publication Data
Chapian, Marie.
    Love and be loved.
    1. Love (Theology) 2. God—Worship and love.
3. God—Love. 4. Christian life—1960–   . I. Title.
BV4639.C42 1983   241'.4   82-18629
ISBN 0-8007-5092-6 (pbk.)

Contents

TO LOVE AND BE LOVED

Part I

The Meaning of Being Loved

You can talk about love until you're blue in the face, but it doesn't mean a thing until you have a personal confrontation with it, until you meet it headlong and can honestly say to love, "Hey, I know you."

Can you and I say we *know* love? In teaching on the subject for the past several years, I have asked people how they think about themselves in the light of God's love. Out of countless Christian audiences around the world, very few men, women, or children have told me they truly live in the experience of God's love daily, or that they tell themselves they're anything precious to God.

To millions of Christians, John 3:16 doesn't have a shred of daily significance. "For God so loved the world ..." is a very fundamental truth, but so often it is not an experiential one. The love I'm talking about in this book is not the emotion that brings forth thoughts of moonlight and violins: no, not romantic love. I'm not talking about wedded bliss, or parent-child love; or even a deep, abiding human friendship. I'm talking about a supernatural, ever-present, all-encompassing, glorious, truly life-giving and life-changing, revitalizing, captivating, eternal love that transcends and makes possible human affection: God's love.

C. S. Lewis was moved by the description of desolation

which Saint Augustine wrote about the death of his friend
Nebridius (*Confessions* 4:10). Saint Augustine drew the
following moral from his painful experience: He said his
grief was the fruit of giving his heart to anything but God,
because all human beings pass away. "Do not let your
happiness depend on something you may lose. If love is to
be a blessing, not a misery, it must be for the only Beloved
who will never pass away."

This is the extreme of which I teach here. Jesus Himself
wept over Lazarus and did not withhold His love for him
just because His friend was human and not God. There
are no insurance policies against heartbreak in the love
kingdom of God. I agree with C. S. Lewis that to love is
to be vulnerable. But to *be* loved is God's foundational
gift to us through Jesus Christ.

We don't throw away natural love; we allow God's love
to permeate our conscious minds and actions until we see
ourselves and live through Him and His love.

It is possible to experience the love of God every day. I
discovered that a person can know without a shadow of a
doubt who he or she is and that he or she is dynamically
important to the Creator of the universe. I have learned
that this knowledge can produce a powerful way of life
hitherto untapped.

Loving and being loved takes work. The German poet
Rainer Maria Rilke tells us in his *Letters to a Young Poet*
that love might just be our most strenuous achievement.
"For one human being to love another: that is perhaps the
most difficult of all our tasks, the ultimate, the last test and
proof, the work for which all other work is but a preparation," he said.

Most people are victims of circumstances, events, situations, and relationships. If things go well, we feel good. If our expectations and demands are met, we feel a sense of gratification. Sadly, too many of us never go further than this plateau of life for our happiness. What happens, then, when events, circumstances, and situations run amok? What happens when demands go unmet, expectations unfulfilled? Neuroses, various physical symptoms of stress, unhappiness, divorce, and even suicide can result.

When a person displays neurotic behavior, he or she can employ several palliative methods to help overcome the disturbance, such as changing jobs or marital status, taking up a hobby, consuming tranquilizers or other drugs, or a variety of diversionary activities. These diversions may help temporarily, but they don't solve problems. Denying that problems exist won't solve them. Running from them won't help.

I have taught the principles of how to live as a Loved Person, and the results in people's lives have been incredible. Learning what to do and how to make it work is the key. As a Christian and a professional psychotherapist, I believe the Word of God provides the finest therapy available.

That's why this book was written. All people and all illustrations are based on real people and real events, though I have changed their names. The poems I've written at the end of each chapter are the first to appear since my books *City Psalms* and *Mind Things* were published.

This is a book for everybody. It doesn't matter who you are or where you are. I promise you, if you will allow the principles set forth here to sink in, you will be a different person. I have yet to see a person who has learned how to be a Loved Person continue to live in defeat.

I am praying for you because I believe in you. Your life is about to explode with beautiful experiences and expressions of yourself. In love you become you.

The greatest contribution I have to offer you is to help you see yourself as loved. If you will accept my gift to you, you will gain what none can take away or alter: your infinite value, uniqueness, and worth. I want to be your friend, to be faithful to and honest with you, and to give only what is true and good in me to you. I want you to see what I see in you. I want you to know how to be a Loved Person so that together we can be something beautiful for God.

1

Who Are You?

My first car was one of the most elaborate displays of wrinkles, dents, bumps, breaks, and rust in our state. I had barely learned how to drive when I bought the car. I didn't mind how it looked. To me, stepping on the gas and hearing the engine was a notable thrill. The heater in the car didn't work, so I had to bundle up my children in blankets in the winter. (I didn't learn to drive until after the children were in school.) The temperatures were twenty degrees below zero, with the windchill factor; and without a heater or a defroster, my windshield would freeze up so I couldn't see a thing in front of me. Sometimes I had to drive with my head hanging out the window to see where we were going. My eyelashes froze once, and it took me an hour and a half to thaw them out. My face would look like a steel-belted radial tire, with ice streaked from forehead to chin. That car was the most amazing vehicle on the street.

Another of its features was that it made so much noise, when I drove in our neighborhood I always felt I should call the neighbors to warn them I was coming. It seemed as if everything was loose on the car. If I kicked the snow from its underside, usually part of the fender would fall off, too. It was full of surprises.

We called this car Revelation (because it had been through everything!). I was speaker at dozens of elegant banquets, luncheons, and dinners; and there I was, pulling into country-club parking lots in dear old Revelation. I received many a disapproving glance when I parked the only car that looked as though it had survived a demolition derby. When I visited friends, I usually asked if they preferred that I park down the block from their house, so their neighbors wouldn't be alarmed. I'm telling you, this car was the sight of the year. A used-car dealer actually had the nerve to ask me, when he looked at Revelation's right side, "Was anybody hurt?"

But my children and I loved that old car. We blessed it every day. We washed it, took care of it, and even took pictures of ourselves standing next to it. I really didn't want to get rid of the car, but when a distinct lack of a notable thrill at the sound of a dead engine became habitual, it was time to say good-bye to dear old Revelation.

My new car just doesn't have the personality Revelation had. My nieces no longer shout, "Aunt Marie must be here!" when passing a junkyard. We're respectable, like everybody else, when driving on the freeway. Not once has anyone broken into unrestrained laughter when I've pulled into a gas station. I don't leave pieces of fender behind me in parking lots anymore. I feel so ordinary.

And here's where I get to the point of the story. The Apostle Paul said, "I know both how to be abased, and I know how to abound: every where and in all things I am instructed both to be full and to be hungry, both to abound and to suffer need" (Philippians 4:12). I was the same person chugging around in old Revelation as I am in a new station wagon or on a commercial airplane, boat, or bicycle.

You're not any more important driving a new car than you were in your old car. You're not any less valuable because you have fifty cents in your pocket and your neighbor has a dollar. Look at your *heart,* and you'll know who you are. All else is secondary.

There was a time when I didn't have one cent for Christmas gifts for my children. I bought my own winter coat for twenty-five cents at Goodwill and got the children's snowsuits on time payments at Sears. There wasn't enough money to buy shoes for the children when they needed them, so I figured out a way to revive the old ones with house paint, cardboard, and colored laces. In only a matter of hours, after drying them in the sun, the girls had shoes good as new.

I wanted to make the birth of Jesus special for the children, and I refused to allow a lack of money to hinder us. I made doll cribs out of crates obtained from the supermarket, and I sewed brightly colored quilts from fabric scraps. On Christmas morning, beside a six-inch-high plastic tree left over from days past, my children discovered their treasures. What a celebration! They couldn't have been happier if I had given them the Hawaiian islands.

Our greatest gift that year and every other year was and is commemorating God's magnificent act of love in sending us our Savior, Jesus. In the time that has passed since the little cribs sat beside the miniature plastic tree, our love and respect for God and each other have grown. We know who our gift is and we know that all we are and have is from His sweet, generous love-hand.

Just recently I was sharing with a friend about that meager Christmas and chuckling about our Christmas dinner of popcorn (we tried stringing it, but ate it instead), pickles, and orange juice. My two daughters, who happened to be listening, looked at me with expressions of utter amazement.

"Mom," they asked later, "you mean we were *poor* that year?"

I had to smile. Only the eyes of love would not have seen how poor we were. "Love is never poor," I said.

We create our own world when we know who we are. Identified with Christ, we're elevated from the miseries of being poor and in continual lack. I absolutely refused to think of us as poor because I knew in Christ we *couldn't* be poor. I looked for richness in everything. I looked for meaningful, wonderful touches of beauty and godliness in all things. I refused bereft, empty thoughts and dreams. I found a wealth beyond description in my children's laughter, in our conversations, in our hugs and kisses. I learned how to be rich during those days, how to be truly rich. And we've stayed rich.

God's principle is that we prosper as our souls prosper. The Lord says He is our shepherd, and therefore, we shall not want. Have you ever wondered why there is such an overwhelming pursuit for money, comforts, more leisure time, beauty, luxuries? The answer is simply that people want to be happy, and these things hold a glimmer of hope to that end.

How wise the person who bypasses these contingencies and heads directly toward happiness without them.

> If you are made happier because of what you have, make certain you could be just as happy with who you are and without what you have.

Take the fellow who works hard to build a business. He gives it his best energies. Then, through no fault of his own, it fails; he's forced to sell out at a loss. What he does about this seeming defeat will prove what stuff he's made of. Will he build another business; will he give up forever?

People confuse what we *do* or *have* with who we *are*. You may be a person of many achievements, with accolades; but can you ask yourself the question *Is heaven impressed with me?* Can you ask, *When God looks at me, whom does He see?*

These questions can only be answered by knowing something about God and His thoughts as He expressed Himself to us through His Word. Before we talk about His thoughts, let's talk about yours.

Know Your Thoughts and You'll Know Yourself

Your life is controlled by your thoughts. These thoughts are open to God. Others may see only how you're dressed, how much weight you've gained or lost, how bald you're becoming, or how well you play handball. Your friends see as much of you as you're willing to reveal. If you want them to see only your sweet, charming, benevolent side, they can only guess at what's missing. If someone is your real friend, you will not be afraid to let your negatives show. A real friend, like Jesus, says, "I know there are negatives but I love you anyway."

I know a professional tennis player who has looks the girls go crazy over. His performance on the tennis court holds men and women spellbound. I was surprised to learn he psyched himself before his matches with violent and destructive self-talk. Once on the court and playing, he cursed every minute of the game. If you heard him, you'd think he was a fighter pilot in the midst of war instead of a nice fellow playing a game of tennis. Still, he is a charmer, and people are attracted to him.

Outward appearance, personality, talent, and ability are tools we all use to enhance our personhood. Perhaps the tennis player has feelings of self-admiration for his social skills as well as his tennis skills. But how much good does his vanity do anybody else? Compare him with Jesus, who was never called a charmer.

Another important point to consider is that people will develop opinions of you, not only according to what you are willing to reveal of yourself, but according to their own interpretations of your behavior; their experience; and most important, their own present needs. If outwardly you appear to be a strong, brave person, and your friend is looking for a strong, brave friend, you may become what he thinks: an answer. You appear to fit the bill, so in you go. Now you are expected to be the person that friend sees you as. You may not be at all what he sees. He is seeing you out of his own need or want.

Henrik Ibsen's play *A Doll's House* is an example of this. Nora is the doll-wife who allowed her husband to invent a version of her that bore no resemblance to her actual character. By her acquiescence, she became his accomplice in the deception. His imagined version of her was less than she really was.

Later in this book I'll discuss some of the roles we play and why. It all begins with what we *think*.

Jesus, the Son of God, as He lived on earth, is our example of the perfect person. He saw Himself as God saw Him. Even on the cross, His thoughts were in accordance with His Father's thoughts: those of forgiveness and compassion. Here was the Perfect Man.

When Jesus was unjustly sentenced to death, His execution was cruel, with no defense. Look at this Perfect Man, beaten horribly, abused, and traumatized. When He hung from nails on a cross, He was so grotesquely distorted in pain that those around Him could hardly bear to look at Him. He was no hero at that moment, no adorable fellow in new sneakers, sporting a smart new tennis racket—no suntanned celebrity, flashing a white smile and wearing cologne and custom-made clothes. He was ugly and repulsive looking. Isaiah wrote in the eighth century B.C. of Christ's agony on the cross: ". . . he hath no form nor comeliness; and when we shall see him, there is no beauty that we should desire him" (Isaiah 53:2).

Our heavenly Father said that in this broken, unsightly, dying man, all the fullness of the Godhead bodily would dwell (Colossians 2:9). Jesus died a humiliating, degrading death; despised, rejected, and forsaken by men and women. This He endured so that you and I, through His death, would be elevated to new life, empowered by His Holy Spirit.

And it is in *this* crucified man that we are made complete. This man of sorrows, acquainted with grief, afflicted and smitten, is the head of all principality and power (Colossians 2:10). It is He who sits at the right hand of God, far above all principality and power, might and dominion, and every name that is named (Ephesians 1:21). It is in Him that you are made alive; in fact, even made to sit with Him in heavenly places (Ephesians 2:6).

You can pray to Him, talk to Him, share with Him, friend to friend, lover to lover. You do not have to be anything to impress Him. All He looks for is your heart and your thoughts. If He has those, He has you.

Your thoughts about self-importance may differ greatly from His. You may see yourself as important and of value if others confirm that by tokens of recognition, awards, and even by choosing you as a friend. When people tell you you're important to them and their happiness, you are naturally more important in your own eyes.

But what if no one tells you you're important? If you reach a place in life where you have nothing, own nothing, are loved by nobody, what do you do?

The Real You

Imagine yourself without a thing. You have no family, no friends, no possessions. Your school friends have vanished. Your job has flown out the window. Your home has evaporated into thin air, along with everything you own and everyone you love. *Who are you now?*

I've read too many books and heard too many sermons teaching me how to understand love through my abilities and through my relationships with other people. For me, love has got to be deeper than this. God's love demands more if we are to really come into the place of oneness with *Him.* This we do without contingencies.

I have often thought of God's love for me in terms of what He did for me, the prayers He answered, the blessings He bestowed. When a prayer was fulfilled, I was certain of His love. But there have been prayers He did not answer. There have been pleas He did not respond to; anguished cries in the night, with no answer. I felt empty, as if I were nothing.

In my nothingness and emptiness I made a quality decision. I decided that I would always and forever see God as He said He is: *love.* It was not a conditional decision. It did not depend upon circumstances.

God has tested this decision. In my darkest hours, I have truly been able to pray honestly, "Thank You, Lord, for loving me perfectly and without error. You see me as precious. You care for me as one of immense value and worth. That is enough for me."

There have been times when it really seemed, outwardly, that God was not on my side at all. I felt no warm assurance such as one receives from a human friend who will give a hug and say something kind. There have been times when I felt none of God's encouragement to go on in trust and faith, and had no sweet feeling of His presence and approval. At those times I said, "Shall I trust feelings or God's Word?" With that, I'd throw back my head and exclaim, "Thank You, Jesus, for loving me!" I'd shout it if I had to. "Lord Jesus, thank You for teaching me how to live as a Loved Person!" You can do this, too, every day of your life. But you must start with your thoughts.

Making a List of Things to Think About

If you're like most people, you make lists of things to do, places to go, people to see, tasks to accomplish. Let's add another list now. This one is probably far more important than all the rest combined, because once you've got this list under control, all the others will fall right into their proper places. Make a list of things to think about. Call it your Think About List.

You could put it right next to your shopping list. There by *milk* and *eggs* you might put Colossians 2:10: "I am complete in Him, the head of all principality and power." During the day you think about the verse, mull it over in your mind, meditate on it, and say it out loud to yourself, over and over again.

If you're a businessperson, you might put your Think About List next to your business-appointment list. Right by "Call Murdock about the Snoot merger," you might have, "A good man out of the good treasure of the heart bringeth forth good things . . ." (Matthew 12:35).

When you wake up in the morning, before checking to see what the weather is, sit up in bed and exclaim, "I am a Loved Person. Loved Person is now waking up!" Then greet the Lord Jesus with words of love such as, "This Loved Person loves You, Lord!" You can begin planning right there, before heading for the bathroom, what your thoughts for the day will be.

This is a perfect time to take hold of your victory in Jesus. "Lord Jesus, I am Your person. I give You myself today. I give You my thoughts. I will love You today with my thoughts! Every thought I give to You."

Bless the supermarket, the garage, the subway, the telephone company, the electric company, the living-room carpet, the laundry, the elevator in the place where you work—the list is unending. The power you have in your grasp by turning your thoughts to prayers is astounding! *Pray without ceasing,* we read in the Bible, and the way to obey that is to turn your thoughts to prayers. "Lord, bless this thought" is the start of it all.

Remember, you're not doing this for favors. You're doing it for the Lord Jesus, so you can love Him more fully and allow His love to totally possess you. You are not expecting to manipulate God. If something happens that you don't like, you aren't going to fall into a heap of despair and complain about how God has failed you. You're not going to lament, "After *all* I've done for Jesus, and now *this!* I've made Think About Lists for three days in a row, and I've been so good. Oh, why won't God bless me?"

God wants to bless you. He loves to bless you! Think of Him as blessing you. He is not interested in hurting you or robbing you of happiness. He will withhold nothing from you.

You really *are* a Loved Person! Realize it! Take it! You can shout it, celebrate it. You never have to take less again; you're on your way to the richest, fullest life you can live as the real you!

When You Feel

When you feel the world shrinking
    like a wet woolen sleeve
      around you
    and you feel life becoming
      a lump of leftovers
in some refrigerator
       ;when you feel that everyone
           you know
      cares less
           about you
    than wild animals
      in another
           civilization:
when looking into a mirror
    feels like
      pins in your nose
    and when you feel there is no place
      in the whole
           fat
           earth
      you'd
      like to be
    that's when it's
      sweetest
      to remember
      God
      in resplendent wonder
      continually sends you
           His
            kiss
           of
           love
,the kind that fills
    seas
    and moves mountains,
      regardless of
        your
          fee
           lings

2

A Different You

Knowing who you are changes you! It can change your whole life. God creates in you a tenderly affectionate and caring heart. Where there once was stone, He gives you the ability to cherish and respect others as well as yourself. Love builds you, renews you, invigorates you, brings you into contact with the world around you. Above all, love builds your opinions and feelings about yourself; it gives you self-esteem.

There have been many studies made of infant growth failure due to maternal deprivation, but I'd like to tell you about one case. A thirteen-and-one-half-month-old girl was brought to the hospital after experiencing an eleven-month period of maternal deprivation. The mother, who was mentally unsound, had been told during the baby's second month that too much attention might spoil her child. The mother then avoided physical contact with the infant in every way possible. She only visited the baby during feeding time. Otherwise the child was left to fend for herself, isolated from all human contact. The baby became inert, grew listless, could not hold down her food; the mother brought her to the hospital, complaining, "There's something wrong with my child." The baby weighed only ten pounds, lay on her back, motionless, and bore an apprehensive expression

26

on her face. Her hands were cupped over her mouth, and she constantly chewed her fingers.

Ninety days later, after a program of intensive mothering, with a single nurse providing most of the attention, the changes in the child were remarkable. The case report read:

> Within days after the mothering program was initiated, the infant's expression brightened; she began to say "mama" to her nurse-mother and started eating well and gaining weight. Several weeks later, she could sit upright without assistance and roll over with good motor control.

Love changes us. René Spitz studied two groups of infants. One group was brought up in a foundling home and not well attended to. They were neglected and given no love. The other group, also institutionalized, were visited every day by a retarded girl who played with them, loved them, and showered them with affection and attention. The first group became maladaptive and unable to finish school; some went to prison; some died. Of the other group, each one graduated from high school and married happily, except one; they adjusted well to life in later years. Love changes us. Somebody must love us, and whether it be a mother, a peer, a nurse, or a visitor, it's necessary if we are going to know how to relate to this world around us. The little thirteen-and-one-half-month-old baby could have died if she had not been brought to the hospital. Cause of death: lack of love.

These examples show us what we are like when we are not in a position where God can shower us with His love. We're listless and staring at life with terrified eyes. We have no appetite and in our isolation, will often mutilate ourselves.

Most of us don't experience the kind of neglect described

above, but as I minister across the land, I meet many people who are emotionally crippled because they do not believe they are lovable. Are you one of these? Are you telling yourself you're not lovable because of your past experiences?

Your Impression of Yourself

A man I'll call Jim had a debilitating self-image problem. His impression of himself was dismal. He wouldn't dream of telling himself he was special or a beautiful person. Jim was a sweet guy and genuinely likable, but he frequently stirred up trouble because of his lack of self-esteem. He constantly demanded compliments from his family and his friends. He continually had to be assured that he was okay.

Jim's self-image depended upon other people's judgments, advice, and responses. He demanded that someone else tell him he was wonderful, handsome, marvelous, witty, clever, frugal, and so on. If no one told him, he simply *wasn't.*

Jim may be a person who can understand and relate to a boy we can name "I. Can't." The boy is six years old and is out in the backyard, trying to throw a baseball to his dad. Dad is training his boy to be a great ballplayer. He throws the ball to his son. I. Can't misses it, and Dad snaps, "For crying out loud, you're not paying attention! Now try again!"

I. Can't tries and misses again. Dad groans, showing his displeasure. "Your sister can catch the ball better than that!"

The little six-year-old feels rotten about himself. Next time Dad offers to play ball, he says, "I can't."

Perhaps you're feeling that you've missed the ball and therefore are less than you ought to be. My friend, you've got the right to miss the ball once in a while—or all the time, for that matter. I. Can't was not under any obligation to

God or man to catch the ball. He tried. He missed. Nothing in the Word of God says we are forbidden to make mistakes or that we *must* meet other people's expectations.

Jim had done well academically because he performed up to the expectations of his teachers. He was an honor student in high school, but he told me he had never thought of himself as a good student or as being particularly bright.

"Nobody *told* me I was smart," he said. "Years after I graduated from high school, I ran into an old classmate who said, 'Oh, yeah, Jim, you were always the brainy one in class.' You can't imagine my shock."

I know a woman who won a beauty pageant once and was amazed. She didn't think she could have won fairly. "It had to have been political maneuvering," she said suspiciously.

"Why do you think that?" I asked.

She said, "My mother always told me I was an ugly duckling."

"But what do *you* tell yourself?" I asked her.

She couldn't answer me. She wasn't yet sure whom to believe. Her own opinion didn't count. Jim couldn't understand why anyone called him smart. Six-year-old I. Can't may never believe he can play a decent game of baseball.

Whose opinion do you value? No matter how many times you have been put down in the past, you can form your own opinion now, based on *God's* opinion: "Yet the Lord will command his lovingkindness in the daytime, and in the night his song shall be with me, and my prayer unto the God of my life" (Psalms 42:8).

Do You Still Think Like a Teenager?

Erik Erikson, the developmental psychologist, suggested that at its best, identity is experienced as a sense of well-being. A person with a secure identity feels at home in his body, knows where he is going, and feels assured of recognition from people who count, to him. As adolescents we seek our sense of well-being through the approval of our peers.

As a teenager I made choices regarding my role as a female in the world by discovering acceptance in behaviors and endeavors that defined me as an okay person. I was applauded and admired for my accomplishments and skills, and I felt, for the most part, acceptable.

But now I am an adult. I no longer find my okayness in my skills or in my acceptance by others. In adolescence there are pressures from three sets of social groups: the family, the peer group, and larger organizations such as the school. We play at least one role in each of these groups. For each of these roles there is a set of role definers—people with whom we interact and who define our roles by indicating appropriate behavior and by supporting and rewarding us when we display it. This is how the teenager comes to judge himself or herself. Appearance, academic achievement, and social capabilities are judged by the standards of those who define the roles in social groups. The dominant influence as role definers are parents, peers, and teachers. It would have been unacceptable for me as a teenage girl growing up in the Midwest to want to be a doctor. It was more acceptable to be a secretary or a nurse.

Our high-school years can be some of the happiest in our entire lives. Adolescence is the first phase in which we begin to carefully think about ourselves and seriously consider our own impressions of ourselves, as well as others' impressions of us. We make plans, rehearse long-range purposes, and develop our processes of choosing our identities and self-concepts during these years.

As a Christian person your self-concept is wrapped up in *God.* The Lord says you have worth and beauty and intrinsic value; His opinions are the ones that count. You need to hear and respond to *Him.*

Teenage behaviors, however, are appropriate for teenagers, not for adults. Prolonged adolescence is your own choice. People are attaining physical maturity earlier and are more educated than ever, but emotional and social maturity lag behind. By clinging to adolescent thought patterns, the adult can live a crippled life, in spite of his or her learning status.

The stages of human development can be experienced, gained from, and fulfilled happily and without turmoil. The Christian teenager can live an exciting, productive life as a Loved Person. The same is true for the Christian child and adult. Our enemy, the devil, wants every stage of our development to be plagued with turbulent storms of self-doubt and misery.

The devil wants a Christian's childhood debilitated and sapped of happiness. He wants our adolescence enervated with feelings of instability and unsubstantiality. He wants us to live an insipid, sin-sick adult life, running in every direction but into the arms of God. The devil is a joyless liar whose poisonous mark is destruction.

Christian person, God has given you power and might to overcome and crush the devil's work in your life!

Using the Power Within You to Change

Jesus said in Acts 1:8, "Ye shall receive *power,* after that the Holy Ghost is come upon you. . . ."

In Luke 4:14 Jesus returned in the power of the Spirit into

Galilee, ". . . and there went out a fame of him through all the region round about."

Matthew 28:18: "And Jesus came and spake unto them, saying, All power is given unto me in heaven and in earth."

Acts 4:33: "And with great power gave the apostles witness of the resurrection of the Lord Jesus: and great grace was upon them all."

Do you suppose you're filled with the Holy Spirit in order to fail? Do you suppose you have received power to do poorly, remain sick, stay defeated? When you become a Christian by giving your life to Jesus Christ, and you receive the baptism of the Holy Spirit, you receive *power*—and for what? Power to remain a thirty-five-year-old teenager? No!

If Jesus has all power on heaven and earth and you are His child, does He use His power to give you a rock when you ask for bread? Does He use His power to give you a snake when you ask for a fish? No! *He gives you His power so you can defeat the devil!*

You're not empowered for failure—you're empowered for winning. You can win over the devil's lies, which tell you you're mediocre, unlovable, not worth much.

You're Jesus' property, and that makes you loved and lovable. You're touched by God. You're blessed by His love and care. You're valuable. You're a beautiful person!

Your personhood is to be found in the Kingdom of God, not in the kingdom of darkness.

The Kingdom of God	*The Kingdom of Darkness*
Love, contentment, happiness, a feeling of well-being and strength to rise above negativity and demonic forces. Power to win.	Nervousness, worry, fear, hatred, bitterness, loneliness, sickness, doubt, hopelessness, self-destructive thoughts and behaviors. Powerlessness.

A woman whom I counseled for several months shared with me how her growing years were the cause for her current neurosis and unhappiness. I attempted to show her this was not true. Certain experiences in our lives may have been painful, but it is not true that these experiences shape our current behavior. What you *think* about these experiences determines your behavior.

My patient learned to change her attitudes, thoughts, and talk regarding her past. "My mother always bragged about how smart I was," she told me, "but now I know I don't have to depend upon somebody else to tell me how smart I am before I believe it myself."

If you are a Christian, you are not conformed to this world, but you are transformed by the renewing of your mind by the Word of God! (Romans 12:2).

You cannot change your past, but you can change the way you *think* about it. You can tell yourself regarding painful experiences: _____ *was painful to me and I experienced hurt and sorrow. Though it was difficult and painful, it will not destroy me and doesn't stand as the worst thing in this world.*

Tell yourself, *I choose to stop telling myself how* terrible *things were. I choose to stop telling myself how* bad *and how* painful *things were. I choose to tell myself this:*

> *Even though I have had experiences that were unpleasant in my life, I am a new person, every single day, in Jesus Christ. I am valuable to Him and filled with wonderful godly potential, brimming with newness and new thoughts and ideas.*

I choose to drop my negative and gloomy thoughts and attitudes about my past experiences. I choose to take my new mind and new heart and live in the world of God's love and hope.

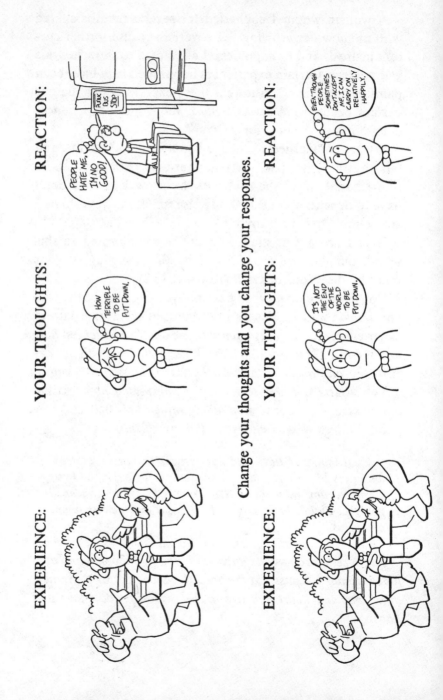

If you can say those words, you are on your way to making your life dynamic. You have proven to yourself that you can change. Your possibilities are limitless because now you see that you really are unique, beautiful, and usable. You are God's Loved Person.

who says?

who says you're not beautiful,
who says you're not loved
?who's the culprit, the slimy toad,
the one without integrity
or honesty in him?
do you know who?
the liar,
the coward
sneaking up apples trees,
deceiving
            destroying;
roaring like a lion in the
night.
turn your face away.
your ears were made
for truth because
in all within and throughout
you're posi
tively marvelous
to God

3

The Importance of What You Say to Yourself

A lady I'll name Minnie told me that the world was passing her by, and nobody cared about her. Her self-image was so low she confided she practically had to stand on a ladder to look in the mirror. She felt and acted as though she was a human mishap, ever putting herself down. She saw herself as a veritable rotten apple in the great fruit salad of life.

Minnie complained that nobody cared about her, but in truth she had many good friends who cared deeply. She had a loving family and a faithful husband who tried hard to satisfy Minnie's demands.

But Minnie was not satisfied. Nothing was going her way, she said.

In this chapter we are going to talk about the words we say to ourselves. In the book *Telling Yourself the Truth,* which I wrote with Dr. Bill Backus, we introduced what we call *self-talk*.

Self-talk is the words we tell ourselves in our *thoughts.* The Bible says, "As a man thinketh in his heart, so he is" (*see* Proverbs 23:7). The thoughts you have will emerge from your mouth, and you will speak them to yourself:

Oh, dumb me.
There I go again, doing something stupid.
Life is passing me by.
Nobody will ever love me.
I'm a loser.
Ridiculous. But these *thoughts* develop into words. Then these words develop into behaviors. These behaviors develop conflicts with others, with your work, and your health. Your self-talk can build your self-esteem or destroy it.

Self-talk means the words you tell yourself about: (1) yourself; (2) others; (3) your experiences in the past and present; (4) God; (5) the future; and (6) life in general.

Specifically, self-talk is *all of the words you say to yourself all of the time.*

Much of your self-talk is loaded with untruth. Instead of sound faith in the truth, it can be cluttered with misbeliefs. (The principles as well as how to apply Misbelief Therapy to your life are thoroughly discussed in *Telling Yourself the Truth* and the *Telling Yourself the Truth Workbook*.)

Minnie's self-talk was based on the misbelief that her life and wants should be of utmost importance, if not the most important thing in the lives of those around her. This misbelief paved the way for self-talk such as:

1. It's terrible when I don't get my own way.
2. It's terrible when people don't behave the way I want them to.
3. It's terrible to be disappointed.

These are misbeliefs because they simply are not true. It is *not* terrible if you don't get your own way. It is *not* terrible if people don't behave as you wish they would. It is *not* terrible to be disappointed. It won't kill you if things go awry. It may be unpleasant, uncomfortable, or undesirable, but it is *not* terrible.

Self-talk that is predominantly "terrible" talk will eventually give you feelings of unhappiness. How can anyone be happy when everything is "terrible"?

I've had experiences in my own life that have been downright devastating. As long as I continued to tell myself how rotten, miserable, and "terrible" things were, they stayed that way.

I am not suggesting that you deny hardship or painful feelings! Far from it! May it never be! Admit to them—but do it in a healthy way.

Yes, I feel bad, but I can carry on anyhow.

My feelings are hurt, but it's okay.

I don't like it that such-and-such happened, and I am unhappy about it. I will, however, trust God and carry on!

The Origins of Your Self-Talk

One of the most often-quoted Scripture verses, and perhaps the one from the famous 1 Corinthians 13 love chapter you immediately recognize, is this:

> When I was a child I was accustomed to speak as a child. I used to understand as a child. I was accustomed to reason as a child. When I have become a man and have the status of an adult, I have permanently put away the things of a child. . . .
>
> 1 Corinthians 13:11 WUEST

We can expect a teenager to act, understand, and speak as a teenager. When he or she becomes an adult, those teenage behaviors and attitudes are "put away," finished or passed through. A child four years old may cry and throw temper tantrums to get his own way, but through learning, we can expect the adult to put away that behavior (you hope) by the time he or she is forty-four years old.

A child of three cringes and buries his head in his sleeve when mother says, "Say hello to our guests," because he's shy and intimidated by strangers. The adult puts away such behavior (although you may see the adult gulping copious amounts of alcohol in order to face a group of strangers or confront an anxiety-arousing situation).

Interestingly, Jesus tells us in Matthew 18:3 that we are to become as little children. If we don't become as little children we can't enter the Kingdom of heaven. Is He contradicting Himself? On one hand we are supposed to put away childish things and on the other we're to become as little children.

Let's differentiate these two admonitions. You and I know there are godly and ungodly behaviors. There is faith, and there is sin. We know that "whatsoever is not of faith is sin." When Jesus said, "Be as a child," He was referring to the child of *faith*. This is the godly person who trusts Him in everything.

The Lord Jesus is impressed with the person of faith who comes to his Master like a loving child and throws himself headlong into God's care, trusting Him implicitly, seeking only to please Him and stay close to Him. This child wants to do just as his Lord does. This child isn't truly happy anywhere else. No matter where he is or what he is doing, he wants his Master there with him.

When, then, do problems arise? If you remain a Christian *child* bearing the responsibilities of an *adult,* you may experience some harsh reactions. You may feel put upon, pressured, critical, unfulfilled, and angry. As a consequence, your behavior may include gossiping, outbursts of temper, prayerlessness, overeating, drinking, crying, sleeping more hours than you need, hateful outbursts, and competing for attention.

Your self-talk may resemble Minnie's:

The world is passing me by.

The work I do isn't really important.

I'm not as valuable as other people are.

These sentences are not true. They are misbeliefs. Let's look at Minnie's background. Somehow, as she has gone along in her Christian walk, she has failed to permanently put away the things of a child.

When Minnie was a teenager she was the pretty, spoiled, only child of a wealthy businessman. She got her own way by whining and by "being cute." Boys were attracted to her cuteness and flirting; teachers were charmed by her. Minnie developed strong manipulative techniques to get her own way. If Minnie wanted a compliment from a friend, she would manipulate for it something like this: "Oh, I'm just a poor little old ugly mouse today."

Her friend would then respond, "Oh, come on, Minnie, you know that's not true."

"It *is* true. I'm just ugly."

"Minnie, you're *pretty!*"

At home, she learned through her relationship with her father that men were people to be manipulated by feminine cuteness, whining, coy behavior, and affection. She would climb onto her father's lap, nuzzle her head against his chin, and whimper, "Daddy, you must not love me."

"Why, Minnie! Daddy loves his little girl!"

"But you're always at that old office of yours. You just work and work, and I never see you."

"Daddy is working so he can buy his little girl nice things."

"Really, Daddy? You know what Rachel's daddy did? He bought her a pony!"

Not too long after, Minnie received a pony of her very own. By winning her father's attention and tenderness through manipulation, Minnie did not learn that she was lovable without manipulating. Her father reveled in his little girl's fawning over him. He paid her handsomely for her manipulative behaviors.

When Minnie grew up, she didn't learn to put away childish ways. She continued the actions and attitudes learned in childhood and adolescence and discovered they didn't work so well for her as an adult. For her, these behaviors were sin.

The charm and beauty of a young, manipulative teenage girl vanished when she practiced them as a middle-aged housewife. In their place were harsh demands, unrealistic expectations, and self-absorption. Minnie couldn't charm her children, and it infuriated her. (Adults who still think and behave in these childish patterns rarely enjoy the company of children, whom they see as a threat and a reminder of their own lack of power.)

Since Minnie couldn't manipulate her children, she frequently coped with disciplinary problems by screaming, bursting into floods of tears, sulking, and even physical illness. The latter was because she had a poorly equipped spiritual arsenal to fight off illness. By being ill she received the attention, appreciation, and revenge she felt she deserved, not only from her children but from her husband, too.

"Now see what you've all done to me. Because of you, I'm sick! If you had done what I wanted you to do, this wouldn't have happened."

Minnie's opinion of herself sank to sublevels. Because the attention she craved wasn't there, she figured she was a failure and a nothing. "Nobody loves me or cares about me," she complained miserably. Her husband dutifully tried to meet her demands, because he genuinely loved her, but he wasn't as accommodating as her father had been. Another sore spot for Minnie was that her friends didn't shower her with compliments when she manipulated for them. The people at church and on the committee she served refused to acquiesce to Minnie's insistence on her own way. Minnie felt trapped and unappreciated.

But she *could* be free. And so can you. You can take what Jesus Christ has done on the cross for you and make it your own personal ticket to freedom. "The Lord is faithful, who shall stablish you, and keep you from evil" (2 Thessalonians 3:3), and He will be faithful to keep you from remaining a child when you could be enjoying life as an adult Christian person.

Let go of the unhealthy behaviors you learned way back when, even if way back when was only yesterday.

Loved Person, you can dare to grow up. You can dare to discard childish, manipulative behaviors. You can get rid of demands and expectations that have been crippling you.

You want to be loved, to feel important and wanted. You have all these as a Loved Person. You can stop manipulating for attention.

Tell yourself these true sentences:

I am not less important than anyone else.

I am precious and unique because I belong to God.

Willingly I come to God, and willingly He blesses me.

The perfection of my human character is in God's love for me.

You are lovable even when you are not being charming, doing good deeds, or having lovely thoughts. *You belong to the Lord Jesus, and He finds you lovable!*

A Different Kind of Fast

I was teaching and speaking in New York a few years ago. One day as I was praying for the services, the Lord impressed me to have the people go on a fast. It would be a different type of fast. It would have nothing to do with eating or not eating. This was a fast to help us prepare to be happy, fulfilled Christians.

When I presented the idea to the people, I wasn't sure how it would be received. *It was a fast where every participant would abstain from putting himself down for ten days.*

I thought the people would fly right into orbit! Imagine not saying one derogatory or negative thing about yourself for ten days!

The following ten days were a combination of ascending and descending glory. Lives were thrown into havoc as people realized how much time and energy was consumed with self-defaming words and actions. And we wonder why we fail. Our relationships, work, health, and prayer life are all affected by what we tell ourselves.

One man told me, "I find myself hardly able to speak at all! I didn't realize that I put myself down so much."

Every night, at the evening service, I would ask for testimonies regarding the fast. There was laughter and tears. We rejoiced, despaired. It was the most difficult fast the people had ever experienced.

"I've gone without food for as long as twenty-one days," a woman shared. "But I didn't suffer the struggles of *this* fast. To tame my appetite isn't as difficult as taming my tongue. *This* is work!"

"It's like dying!"

"It's changing my whole world."

"I can see how cruel I have been to myself."

"My words were so hateful. I didn't even realize it!"

"Not putting myself down is like having withdrawal symptoms!"

Another woman put her arms around me and cried as she told me, "Oh, Marie, I don't know how to *think* without a put-down. I don't know how to speak without saying something negative about someone or something. The one I put down most is *myself.* What am I going to do?"

At the end of ten days there was not one person out of several hundred who had not broken the fast. Many of these people were mature, dedicated Christians. Taking part in this fast were church leaders, Sunday-school teachers, Bible-study leaders, and ministers. Each of us failed to keep the fast for ten days. At every failure we realized how much more of God we needed.

I could break down the types of destructive self-talk into three categories. Most common were the *"I'ms"*:

"I'm so fat!"

"I'm so thin!"

"I'm so dumb!"

"I'm no good."

"I'm so poor!"

Then there were the *excuses.* Many people broke their fast with sentences like:

"The reason I have a bad temper is that I'm Italian." (Or French or German or whatever.)

"I'm nervous lately because of him." (Or her or them or theirs, and so on.)

"It's just the way I am."

"Other people get all the breaks."

And last, the pitiful, woebegone, *"I don't haves"*:

"Other people are more fortunate than I am."

"When God dealt out looks [or talent or brains, and so on] He sure passed me by."

"I don't have as many friends as other people do."

"I don't have enough love." (Or attention or compliments or admiration.)

God's gift to you is power over yourself and your negative self-talk. All of the above lead to false conclusions.

I'm so fat. I feel bad. I must be bad.

Other people get all the breaks: I must be a loser.

Other people look better and are smarter than I am, therefore I am no good.

Love Changes Your Self-Talk

Our fast, abstaining from negative self-talk, is a vivid representation of how much we lack in knowledge of God's love for us. Knowing something and living it are two different things.

Love is power. As you continue to study and apply the message I'm sharing with you in this book, you will notice yourself changing. Love never fails. Every neurosis you name will fall away one day, but love remains. God is love and as He is in the world, so are you (1 John 4:17). When you know and live in the love of God, your thought patterns are permeated with truth.

Minnie took a good look at herself in the light of the Word of God and changed her self-talk. She saw that God considered her *precious*. She saw she could trust Him with her life and all it contained. She began to tell herself, "I am a Loved Person!" She woke up in the morning and exclaimed, "Hello, Lord, Loved Person is now waking up!" It was less than a year before her entire countenance and personality changed.

Understanding who you are can be the beginning of a totally new life for you, too.

words

the words i hear are
stars
flickering,
millions of them, some shining
brightly, others
dead and falling to the
ground. O
i love you, Lord,
this i know,
and if my words are a link to You
i will
ride them tirelessly upward,
                           upward,
on the blades of gold You say
slice worlds apart.
into the core of You i plunge,
too deep to escape
the surety of Your everlasting
love promise. You, Living Word,
alive and true,
i believe
You.

4

Choosing What You Want in Life

To this point, we've covered some life-changing facts about you. By now you are aware that as God's Loved Person, knowing who you are, accepting yourself, and being in control of your self-talk are vital to your happiness. Now I want to consider another vital point. As God's Loved Person you can learn how to make important choices, possibly the very choices you've never been able to make until now.

Happiness reaches the point of something called *blessedness*. It has something within itself which goes beyond ecstasy and sorrow. At the center of its blessedness is the Savior Himself, providing the very foundation of life. What do you want in life?

Happiness Is a Choice

You and you alone live in your body. You and you alone walk with your head, your thoughts, and your prayers. You and you alone decide whether or not you're going to be a happy person.

I have found that what some people want in the first place is wrong for them. They chose it perhaps because someone else made the choice first. This is wrong for them and causes them tremendous unhappiness. Neurotic people are often not capable of doing something good for themselves. Dr. Allan Fromme says in his book *The Book for Normal Neurotics* that if we don't do all we can for ourselves *without* help from others, there's a very good chance we won't do all we can for ourselves *with* the help of others. Release yourself from the misbelief that happiness is attained through another person.

Since you must deal with your own problems, *you* are ultimately going to have to learn to solve them. It is not necessary to understand a problem before you do something about it. You need to learn to make a habit of *doing* something about your problems. And when your solutions work, repeat them over and over again. This builds the self-esteem we talked about in chapters 2 and 3. You may not have self-esteem because you don't succeed at something. This is different from doing what is expected of you by other people. It is different from doing what you think others want you to do. It is different from struggling silently along, biting your tongue, gritting your teeth, and allowing others to determine your personhood.

A few years back, I was holding a series of meetings in a town in Iowa. Before a morning session, a cynical-looking woman approached me at the platform. She was obviously distressed. "I think you make too much of happiness," she shrilled. "Are you going to talk about happiness today?"

The question took me by surprise; but looking at her, I could see how her heart was hurting. She was trembling with anger.

"Because life is not always *supposed* to be happy," she snapped. "If you were honest, you'd admit it."

She looked so pathetic, standing there trembling with her hurts and bitterness.

"Will you stay close to me during this meeting?" I asked her. "I want to keep my eye on you."

She was taken aback at my response, but she complied and sat right in front of my nose, in the front row. I smiled at her often as I taught the lesson, so she'd know I wasn't forgetting about her. I saw her countenance soften as I spoke.

I talked that morning about a woman who had at one time in life been without much hope for the future. I told about how she had lost her husband and had no way to survive. She had no way to make a living, and remarriage wasn't an option. With the mother of her dead husband, this woman left her own country and people, although she had absolutely no assurance of a happier future.

Talk about reasons to be unhappy—Ruth had them. Of her story in the Bible, the German writer Johann von Goethe said, "We have nothing so lovely in the whole range of epic and idyllic poetry." It is a story born in tragedy (the deaths of her husband, brother-in-law, and father-in-law); it's nourished with biting poverty and hopelessness; and in it develops a deep trust and love between Ruth and her mother-in-law. No more beautiful a commitment of love and faithfulness has ever been spoken than Ruth's to her husband's mother: "Intreat me not to leave thee, or to return from following after thee: for whither thou goest, I will go; and where thou lodgest, I will lodge: thy people shall be my people, and thy God my God" (Ruth 1:16).

Love makes us happy in the absence of hope. Of the three abiding assets—faith, hope, and love—love is the greatest.

The presence of it and the beauty of it is happiness that reaches beyond the limits of hope. The future may have looked grim for Ruth and Naomi, but they had what no situation, circumstance, or event could take away from them: love for each other and for God.

True happiness is built on simplicity. Though the circumstances of the lives of these two widows seemed complicated and terrible, love was simple. "Where thou diest, will I die, and there will I be buried: the Lord do so to me, and more also, if ought but death part thee and me," said Ruth (verse 17).

What Does It Mean to Be Happy?

Choosing what you want in life means that sooner or later you will have to interpret what the word *happiness* means to you. One person may say happiness is contentment. Another says it's feeling good at the moment. Another says happiness is being appreciated. Still another may confidently say that happiness is knowing things such as "God is love!"

At one time, I may have said happiness was the absence of pain, but I believe now that it can be more than the absence of pain. I see happiness as being locked in the embrace of the lover of my soul, the Lord of Hosts. This embrace carries me and lifts me up to heights of happiness I could hardly dream of reaching through my own abilities.

"Behold, I have graven thee upon the palms of my hands ..." (Isaiah 49:16) He sings to us as He carries us along in His love. He rejoices over us with singing, and as we accept His love songs, we become one with His words and one with Him.

God is love, and His words of love to you are from His love-heart, which seeks only the highest and best for you. God had His love-eye on Ruth as she contentedly gleaned in the fields, finding something for her and Naomi to exist on. God blessed her beyond her expectations. Ruth was in a strange country, had pledged herself to a strange God, and was learning strange customs. She had forsaken all to follow Naomi, her beloved mother-in-law.

Ruth's fidelity is a picture of the person who enters a new life in Christ. When Ruth marries rich and successful Boaz, her story forever typifies the love of the Lord Jesus for His own people. Boaz represents Jesus, the Redeemer. Ruth represents the believer. Ruth could never have guessed that her story would be told for generations and that she would be the great-grandmother of the great King David!

Though rejected and hopeless in her own land, Ruth was utterly irresistible to Boaz of Bethlehem, who loved her on sight. He married her, cherishing, respecting, protecting, and loving her.

Reading the story of Ruth in the Bible is a thrill because the Bible is the most realistic of all books ever written. It is the most down-to-earth, the most illuminating, glorious, horrendous, simple, complex of all books ever written. It is our living word link with God. In it are the keys to the substance of happiness.

I told Ruth's story in the church in Iowa because I especially wanted the unhappy woman in the front row to hear it. She had failed at many of her life choices. She did not see herself as lovable to God. For her, simply telling herself she was a Loved Person was not enough. It's not enough for any of us. My children know I love them, but unless they receive that love and the benefits of the love I have for them, it doesn't do them much good. *Love always expresses itself, but it must be accepted.* When the Loved Person reaches out his or her arms of acceptance and takes the love offered, it then has the opportunity to become something great and beautiful.

Suppose you had a craving for carrots and all you had were carrot seeds. In the packet of seeds there could potentially be more carrots than you could use in a year, but they are no good to you unless you plant them in soil that accepts them.

I love being a mother because my children allow me to lavish them with love. They don't suppress my gift of love. All I give them, they happily receive and enjoy. They have blessed me, prayed for me, thanked me, appreciated me, and of course, I'm then encouraged to give more love. Marriage teaches you to die to self, and being a parent finishes the job. Marriage and child rearing will show you how profoundly and unselfishly you can love, or you'll discover the reverse.

I see Ruth as an essentially unselfish woman. Her love and loyalty for her mother-in-law surpassed all else, even her national, religious, cultural, and family bonds.

Oh, the personality of love! Love is loyal. This loyalty defies fear. Naomi's other daughter-in-law, Orpah, wouldn't leave their country of Moab to journey to Naomi's country because she was afraid of what might happen to her there. But loyal, steadfast love is like a roaring wind that hurls fear into a ditch at the side of the road. Ruth loved Naomi, *period.*

Fear has *no* place in the love-heart. "Though he slay me, yet will I trust in him," Job said bravely but foolishly (Job 13:15). Love does not slay its own, of course, though it was a noble thought. Job believed love was worth dying for and his life proved it was truly worth living for.

Instead of running from love, hiding from it, denying it, lying about it, or being afraid of it, you and I can *unite* with it. This love God gives to us may include pain as well as pleasure. Happiness is transcending both. Your love doesn't waver through either. Let us accept this treasure.

God wants a relationship with us. If we are selfish, worried, fearful of our own skins, we might never learn that God is a tenderhearted, loving, good, and merciful God. We don't realize He likes being happy, too. He likes it very much when we purpose in our hearts to bless Him, to make *Him* happy.

That morning in the church in Iowa, we prayed that the Lord would give each of us a relationship with Him that makes *Him* happy.

My friend in the front row had been seeking happiness in the wrong places. She thought happiness came through circumstances or events; she had looked for happiness in friendships, love affairs, and a marriage she lost to divorce. Now she found she had run out of places to look for happiness, and so concluded life isn't happy.

I share this experience with you because it touched my heart so deeply. At the end of the session that day, there were tears running down her face. She told me later, "Marie, God has done the impossible. I've been so messed up." She told me as we talked together, "I really believe I'm ready to be a happy person." She was on her way to change.

The story doesn't end there, because about a month later I received a cassette tape in the mail from the same woman. On the tape she sang about fifteen songs of love which she had written to the Lord Jesus. I listen to that tape often and feel warmth and joy, knowing she has found her real self in the love-heart of God.

What Makes God Happy?

How happy the parent is when a child receives that parent's love. How happy the husband whose wife trusts his love and loves him back. How much more does the Lord re-

joice when we receive and trust the love He loves to give us!
He does not want to withhold any good thing in His Kingdom from us. ". . . it is your Father's good pleasure to give
you the kingdom" (Luke 12:32).

One way to make God happy is to see yourself as He sees
you.

When you finally see yourself as God sees you, His blessings overrun your life. You are no longer interpreting life's
events according to the standards set around you by the
world. You're listening to what God has to say about things.
In this way He is blessing you from the inside out.

You feel so loved. You tell Him, "I will bless the Lord at
all times: his praise shall continually be in my mouth"
(Psalms 34:1).

By blessing the Lord, you become blessed. David said in
Psalms 5:12 (AMPLIFIED), "For You, Lord, will bless the
[uncompromisingly] righteous [him who is upright and in
right standing with You]; as with a shield You will surround
him with good will (pleasure and favor)."

Seeing yourself as a Loved Person gives you a greater ca-
pacity to bless the Lord. There is no doubt in your mind
about your place in His heart.

David tells us in Psalm 100, a psalm of thanksgiving,
". . . Be thankful and say so to Him, bless and affectionately
praise His name!" (verse 4 AMPLIFIED). In blessing God, you
begin to understand His ways and His thoughts.

Psalm 1 shows us how we bless God and how He blesses
us back: "Blessed is the man that walketh not in the counsel
of the ungoldly, nor standeth in the way of sinners, nor sit-
teth in the seat of the scornful" (verse 1). Let's continue by
looking at the next verses.

It's very difficult to busy myself blessing the Lord and at
the same time follow the advice and counsel of ungodly

people, taking their motives and plans for my own. It's impossible to bless and affectionately live a life of praise to God while I stand submissive and inactive in the path where sinners walk. It is not possible to expect the fullness of the blessing of the Gospel of Christ if I'm plunking myself down to have a good time relaxing with mockers of God and people who scorn His ways. Ridiculous. I choose to bless the Lord.

Your life becomes rich and full when you actively pursue and dedicate yourself to blessing God. In return, He literally showers you with His blessings! As it says in the first psalm, you become like a tree firmly planted and tended by the streams of water, healthy and always ready to bring forth fruit in season. Your leaves don't wither, dry up, or fade, bleach, and yellow. Everything you do prospers and comes to maturity. The Lord knows you and is fully acquainted with your ways. He loves you and has sweet, pure fellowship with you. You will always prosper in His blessings when you are in this right place with Him. You're His beloved, held in His arms, closely, lovingly; you are *truly* blessed.

You Make Yourself Happy

The Bible is filled with stories of people who have turned horror into glory. Who is it, then, who tells us we are born to suffer, to live lives of pain or of "quiet desperation"? Why should we suppose that it is our lot in life to dwell in and think in negatives, negatives, negatives? I actually know Christians who fellowship around negatives. They get together every week and talk about how horrible the world is. To these people, sin is everywhere.

A lady once said to me, "I have sinners living next door to me."

I said, "Dear, you have a sinner sitting next to you."

The Bible says we are all sinners *saved* by grace. I'm saved from the power of sin in my life. I want to dwell on the Jesus within us and the power to *overcome* sin. I want to think about "greater is He that is in me than he that is in the world." I want to think about "I have called you with an everlasting love." I want to think about "if any person is in Christ he or she is a new person."

It's the enemy of God who robs you of your happiness. Satan is a joy robber, a faith robber, and a love robber. He steals anything he can from you that's good, beautiful, and true. He wants you miserable, sick, and mean. But Satan is *not* your king. Jesus is your King! Say these sentences out loud:

- I've been taken from Satan's kingdom and am now in God's Kingdom (Colossians 1:13, 14).
- I'm a part of the body of Christ, and Satan has no power over me (1 Corinthians 12:14–27).
- Satan flees from me because I resist him in Jesus' name (James 4:7).
- God has given me power over all the power of Satan (Luke 10:19).
- My eyes have turned from darkness to light and from the dominion of Satan to God (Acts 26:18).

The Blessing of Staying His Friend

The best of all possible blessings is that He reveals Himself to us and tells us in Psalms 25:14 (AMPLIFIED), "The secret [of the sweet, satisfying companionship] of the Lord have they who fear—revere and worship—Him, and He will show them His covenant, and reveal to them its [deep, inner] meaning."

"Henceforth I call you not servants; for the servant

knoweth not what his lord doeth: but I have called you friends; for all things that I have heard of my Father I have made known unto you" (John 15:15).

What is the best possible blessing? To be called a friend of Jesus.

C. S. Lewis said, "There are two kinds of people: those who say to God, 'Thy will be done,' and those to whom God says, 'All right, then, have it your way.' "

Your way is usually not God's way because the purely human expression of love and goodwill is horribly inept next to the spiritual. When you change and make your will and God's will one and the same, you are choosing spirit over carnal, or to put it better, you are choosing the Holy Spirit over your human soul (intellect, emotions, and will). The Word of God teaches us it is the Spirit that giveth life.

Your emotions and human thinking and human will simply do not give life! Only God's Spirit does! You will see unhappy Christians who are oppressed living in the realm of the soul-dominated life. These Christians may be driven by intellectuality, sensuality, or both. In order to be a friend of Jesus, you have to be led and filled with the Holy Spirit of God.

Jude says in the nineteenth verse that there are men who separate, who cause divisions—*worldly minded, devoid of the spirit.* This means devoid of the Holy Spirit of God.

You have a human spirit, and it's capable of lots of nice things. Your human spirit can be noble, brave, kind, giving, and good. But that is not enough. Unless your human spirit is regenerated and indwelt by the Holy Spirit of God (through the blood of Jesus Christ), it is in danger of being in accord with fallen spirits. There are many false religions such as Christian Science, Science of the Mind, and others, that are in accord with fallen spirits. This is the same spirit realm as mediums, clairvoyants, occultists, psychics, witches, and sorcerers. Evil spirits are very real and terrible, but they are cunning and clever enough to convince a person that they are good. They can even convince a naive person they are spirits sent by God. The "soulish" person, or one who is predominantly led by self-vaunting emotions, thoughts, or desires, may fall into the talons of these devious evil spirits. He or she is easily flattered, tempted, and deceived.

There are many soulish persons in the churches today. These are people who are led by selfish thoughts, feelings, and desires, instead of the Holy Spirit. God is aware of this problem and wants us to respond to the Apostle Paul's advice to give ourselves, in every aspect of our lives, to the Holy Spirit. Galatians 5:16 in the Amplified Version of the Bible reads:

> But I say, walk and live habitually in the (Holy) Spirit—responsive to and controlled and guided by the Spirit; then you will certainly not gratify the cravings and desires of the flesh—of human nature without God.

The human spirit was created by God to be indwelt by His Holy Spirit. To be a Christian is to receive God's Spirit into our own. We receive Jesus Christ and all He is into our very beings. His Spirit then becomes ours.

Then *He* can say to *us,* "All right, have it your way," because now He knows our way has fully become His way. We are the few of His children who keep Him busy night and day performing His will by answering our prayers and doing as we ask. "If ye abide in me, and my words abide in you, ye shall ask what ye will, and it shall be done unto you" (John 15:7).

We can define a blessing as Jesus Himself. All that we

have and all that we are is through, in, because of, and with Him. We are blessed as His friends because we bless Him.

In all of life on earth and hereafter, there is no greater blessing than this.

see how Love

cares for us.
　　　　see
　　　　His
　　　　tenderness:
as skies carrying the rains,
　　　　holding the thunder
　　　　and the clouds,
　　　tender is
　　　His love.
　　　tender as the skies.
see how Love
cares for us.
　　　　see
　　　　His
　　　　singing heart,
　　　　　His face so
　　　　　　　　stern
　　　　　　　　loyal
　　　　　　　　laughing
　　　　　　　　sober
　　　　　　　　　O He loves us
.He sings
　　　with us
　　　　　watches
　　　　　waits
　　　　　desires
　　　and you & i
　　　are His happiness
　　　　　　　.He is
　　　　　　　lovely as
　　　　　　　a sun-filled summer day; fierce
　　　　　　　　as oceans shouting
　　　　　　　　to the dawn,
see
how He holds
in the palm of His hand
our sweetest prayers,
　　　　　　　"where you go I will go
　　　　　　　　where you live I will live . . ."
　　　　　　and He loves us loyal
　　　　　　　　beyond forever.

5

The Joy of Having Self-Control

A lady wrote me recently and said, "Marie, please pray for me. I just can't seem to get self-control in my life. I'm sad all the time. It's just so depressing not to have self-control."

Overweight persons have come to me in the hope of getting thin by prayer alone. "Please pray for me, Marie," an overweight person requests. "Pray I'll lose thirty-five pounds by June because I'm getting married in June." (Three weeks from now.)

Being and living love is to agree with God. "Yes, Lord, I am Yours. I am wonderfully made. I *am* precious. You say so and I *am*. I love myself because You love me! I choose to be happy and blessed. I refuse to hurt myself because I am too precious and too wonderfully made."

It's uncanny how the devil influences us. We can actually like and pursue the devilish junk that God says is a no-no.

A heavyset lady tells me she's planning to have her jaws wired shut to stop eating.

An overweight young man tells me he's going to have stomach-bypass surgery. He is also afraid he is developing a drinking problem. "It started with a glass of wine at dinner when I got home from work. Then it became two or three glasses. When I told somebody at work I was afraid I was becoming an alcoholic, he laughed at me. I'm drinking more than ever now."

It is necessary for me to explain that along with prayer, there has to be action. Without action, prayer can't be effective.

We can avoid *doing* by praying and expecting God to work some sort of magic, without any of our own effort or assistance. We expect Him to suddenly zap us—*whammo*—and the drinking problem is gone, the cigarette industry is kaput; macadamia nuts and avocados are no longer fattening, and all lust is gone.

"Well, God can do *anything!*" a chubby young woman grumbles between bites of pecan pie. "He can do anything He wants to, right? He can change my desires, then. Let Him take away my desire to overeat."

In other words, the responsibility for her weight problem is God's. One man told me, "If God didn't want me to be an alcoholic, He could have made me so I hated the taste of liquor."

It's all God's fault?

I was the speaker at a series of revival meetings in Southern California, and one night one of the workers called an hour before the meeting to say he couldn't make it to the church that night. The fellow in charge asked why not. "Well, you see," was the lazy man's reply, "if God had wanted me there, He would have sent somebody to give me a ride; but He didn't, and so I'm not going."

How often we put the blame for *our* irresponsible behavior on God! He's there with power and might and victory in His hands; and we're off in the snares of our feelings, hanging on to selfishness and lack of self-control. It didn't occur to this man to take the initiative to call someone for a ride.

We're begging God, "Please *do* something with me, God." He's saying, *Do it yourself. You have My spirit within you!*

Jesus told us, ". . . if you have faith as a mustard seed, you shall say to this mountain, 'Move from here to there,' and it shall move; and nothing shall be impossible to you" (Matthew 17:20 NAS).

What you need, He said, is faith. "I have given you power to become the sons of God!"

He doesn't need the power to become anything; He already *is* all power and everything. It's *you* who needs the power, and He is giving it to you! "Behold, I give unto you power to tread on serpents and scorpions, and over all the power of the enemy: and nothing shall by any means hurt you" (Luke 10:19).

Some of the deadliest serpents and scorpions are your own destructive choices. You can say to them, "Move from here!" And in the mighty name of Jesus, they will have to move. Many times your lethargy will stand in the way of answered prayer.

> Faith says, "I will, by my life choices, prove the Word of God is true."

Faith is:

1. To believe the Word of God is true.
2. To love yourself in the godly sense of the word, without pride or false humility, but with integrity and honest self-respect.
3. To act on that belief and love.

I recognize times in my own life when I have run away

from the law of love and not acted in faith. I have taken the easy route (fear) and settled into laziness (doubt) and then wondered why my prayers (complaints) weren't answered.

Fear of rejection or failure is a shabby excuse for doing nothing. Self-control is more than saying no to yourself, your fears, doubts, and complaints; it's saying yes to God.

Yes, Lord, I'll trust You and Your Word.

Yes, Lord, I'll cherish myself because You do.

Yes, Lord, I'll choose those things that will bless You!

We can plead with God for victory over compulsive behaviors, but we really need to stop pleading and start learning what God says in His Word. When developing self-control, a daily diet of the Word is vital. Too often we think a prayer will do what only *we* can do by the power of the Holy Spirit and the Word of God.

An evangelist who was once overweight told me that whenever he was tempted to overeat, he realized it was the Word of God he really craved, not the food. So he changed his appetite from fattening food to the Word of God. It was difficult, but it changed his life.

The Word of God produces delight in itself. It also produces faith. If it's self-control you need, saturate yourself in the Word of God. Combined with prayer, you've got mighty weapons to use against the enemy who wants to defeat you with your own appetites and lusts.

Recently I prayed with a girl who was having nightmares and bouts of depression. There were several causes, but one self-destructive behavior I discovered was that she was listening to rock music all day long. She told me, "I don't want to give up the rock music. I *like* it."

Of course you like the thing you need self-control over, or it wouldn't have a strong hold over you. If you didn't like candy, you wouldn't need self-control over the temptation to eat it. If you didn't like the flattery and attention of a non-Christian romantic interest, you wouldn't need self-control to say no to it.

The rock music was hurting the young girl more than she realized. The words, beat, loudness, and satanic spirit of some of the songs were dragging her downward at a fast rate. She had to learn to love herself so she wouldn't defeat and abuse herself. Robert Schuller says loving yourself may be the most important challenge of your life. "Love yourself or die," he says.

Radical? Maybe not.

Faith says, "I can do all things through Christ who strengthens me." Love says, "I trust You, Lord."

Doubt says, "You do it, Lord. I'll just sit back and wait for You to do something for me." Self-control says yes to faith and action, no to doubt and lethargy.

We think of self-control as something of value when we want to give up jelly beans for Lent or when we hold our tempers or when we say no to second helpings. Self-control begins before the action. It begins with our thoughts.

Are you thinking *faith* words?

Self-Control and Your Thoughts

Some time ago a man was convicted on several child-molestation charges. He had a good job, was married, and had two children of his own. His neighbors said he was a likable fellow. He kept his lawn mowed, gave to charities, was friendly. An average guy, they said.

That he was an alleged pedophile and suspected of murder was a shock to all who knew him. Even his wife hadn't suspected her husband's crimes.

How could this seemingly average guy commit such atrocities against small children? The psychologists who interviewed him in the prison where he was held before trial discovered something significant. It came down to this: He thought about doing them. In this case, for years the perverted thoughts had festered in his mind. They corrupted his mind until his conscience was no more. His lust, like a cancer, permeated his thoughts and heart. The causes of the deviant behavior could be traced to his reactions to events in his life and his accompanying thoughts.

The man lusted in his heart and then performed those lusts. He thought in his mind and then acted out those thoughts. He destroyed many lives by actions incited by thoughts.

> There is nothing you do without a thought preceding it.

You are not a victim of some mysterious phantom forcing you to sin, like the fictional tormented character helplessly transformed from a man to a raging monster. You've seen the old movies where a meek and mild-mannered fellow is suddenly stricken by some weird accident of fate. He stands by as his hands turn into hairy claws, while his mouth sprouts tiger's fangs, and with no will of his own, off he bounds, howling in the night, now a hairy, wild beast seeking prey.

Life just doesn't work that way. In the case of demon possession, the thoughts of a person are corrupted and debauched by inhabiting evil spirits. Demons must obtain a way into a person before they can inflict their virulent poison and attempt to possess them. That path is through the mind.

You are a person of control. There are three controls you can choose:

- the control of the Holy Spirit
- the control of the flesh and carnality
- the control of the devil

When you hear words such as, "That behavior was the flesh," or "I acted in the flesh," it means the behavior was earthly, selfish, and unlike God. The same is true of carnality. It's "of the flesh," something that dies without God to give it life. When you are dominated by the devil, you have opened yourself up to letting evil demons take residence. The power of the devil and the flesh are enemies of God. Your mind was created to be infused with the brightness and glory of God. Your mind was created to possess the mind of Christ! "For to be carnally minded is death; but to be spiritually minded is life and peace" (Romans 8:6). "Let this mind be in you, which was also in Christ Jesus" (Philippians 2:5).

The Bible clearly tells us how valuable our thoughts are. We are admonished to watch over our thoughts and gain control of them. "Do not eat the bread of a selfish man [one with an evil eye], Or desire his delicacies; For as he thinks [reckons in his soul] within himself, so he is . . ." (Proverbs 23:6, 7 NAS).

A person *thinks* about something before doing it. You *thought* about reading this book before you started reading it. You *thought* about going to work or staying home; you *thought* about watering the petunias, studying for the math exam, calling a friend on the telephone, paying the bills, or eating the macadamia nuts.

You will do and become as you think. It's important to

know that your moods do not rule your thoughts. It's the other way around. Your thoughts govern your moods. Dr. David Burns, in discussing the principles of cognitive therapy, said, "Twisted thinking is the exclusive cause of nearly all emotional suffering."

The Bible said thousands of years ago in the words of Solomon, "As a man thinketh in his heart, so he is" (*see* Proverbs 23:7).

Think the Word. You can shape the Word of God within your consciousness as you meditate upon it, walk it, and talk it. You will gain self-control; that is, control of yourself so that your *self* will choose God's thoughts and God's ways through His Word. As a Christian you already possess self-control abilities through the power of the Holy Spirit. Part of the fruit of the Holy Spirit is self-control. It's a natural fruit, dripping off the branches of the tree of the Holy Spirit within you.

How to Do It

How do we gain control of thoughts? When we fight doubt and unbelief, what weapons do we use?

The Bible tells us that Loved Persons have all sufficiency in all things and abound to all good works. We are enriched in everything to all bountifulness (2 Corinthians 9:8, 11).

The Bible tells us in Hebrews 4 that the Word of God is sharper than any two-edged sword. So let's use it!

The following is a self-control plan of warfare:

1. Realize your thoughts. Listen to your thoughts or self-talk and *recognize what you are telling yourself.* Your unhappiness is self-created. It is not true that you cannot control or change your feelings and thoughts and emotions. You can say no to yourself and yes to God.

2. Remove the counterfeit self-talk. This is where you literally *refuse* those uncontrolled, lying thoughts. You shout, "No!" to helpless, hopeless words and thoughts. No! No! No! Some sentences you might employ are:

"I am Christ's and my flesh, its affections and lusts are crucified with him" (Galatians 5:24).

"I put on the Lord Jesus Christ and refuse to make provision for my old flesh or to fulfill the lusts of it" (Romans 13:14).

"I choose to walk in the Spirit and therefore, I shall not fulfill the lusts of the flesh" (Galatians 5:16).

"I will let no sin reign in my mortal body, nor will I obey it in its lusts" (Romans 6:12).

3. Replace all words and thoughts of defeat and hopelessness with the truth. You are now combining steps one and two and powerfully exclaiming the truth. You tell yourself, "Yes, I *can* quit biting my nails. Yes, I *can* lose weight. Yes, I *can* stop cursing. Yes, I *can* stop being shy. Yes, I *can* quit smoking. I can! I can! I can!"

Martha T. is sick in bed with a migraine headache. Someone she hardly knew called her stupid. She is maligned, wounded, appalled, and furious.

"Why, she hurt me terribly," she frets, through her pain.

Martha is incorrect. She hurt *herself* terribly.

It doesn't matter what people say about you. They could call you the most terrific thing to hit this world since hubcaps, and if you didn't agree with them and believe what they said was a compliment, you wouldn't feel any better. If somebody calls you dumb, handsome, pretty, mean, fat, stupid, gorgeous, brilliant, talented, it's not the words that affect you. It's what you *believe* about those words.

Martha believes it is terrible for anyone to put her down in any way. If she is called stupid, then she is either misunderstood (a terrible sin) or she is condemned to everlasting stupidity because her stupidness has been discovered.

Self-control refuses such beliefs. Self-control says, "If I should say, 'My foot has slipped,' Thy lovingkindness, O Lord, will hold me up. When my anxious thoughts multiply within me, Thy consolations delight my soul" (Psalms 94:18, 19 NAS).

You can have self-control over indecorous, wrongful sensitivity. There are two kinds of sensitivity. One is the self-toward, self-centered sensitivity that views the world through the eyes of "I." The other is godly sensitivity, led by the Holy Spirit, toward other people and their needs. One is a perverted, devilish drive; the other is a gift of God, rich in love and peace.

The devil perverts God's perfect will with lying counterfeits. The counterfeit says, "Oh, poor me. So-and-so is talking about me again, I just know it. Nobody likes me. I'm ugly and unattractive and dumb."

Boldfaced lies, directly from the pit of hell.

Self-control fights back with prayer power: "I don't like it when so-and-so says unkind things. I'm praying in the name of Jesus that such words will stop." Self-control says, "I'm strong in Christ Jesus!"

Your feelings reflect your thinking, but your feelings are not facts. You can handle negative events that come your way, and choose against ungodly sensitivity. When you experience genuine hurt because of a loss or disappointment, you can handle it! Don't allow your thoughts to be distorted and exaggerated by the devil's perverted sensitivity.

You're not a victim of habits and bad choices any longer! Just because you have failed in the past does not mean you cannot succeed now! You *will* succeed! You will *not* fail!

Say the words out loud that apply to you.

"Yes, I can stop doubting the Word and power of God!"

"Yes, I can read the Word and pray believing every single day!"

"Yes I can stop overeating!"

"Yes, I can give up self-pity!"

"Yes, I can stop blaming others for my problems!"

"Yes, I can stop drinking!"

"Yes, I can stop smoking, even though I have been smoking for years!"

"Yes, I can stop lusting!"

"Yes, I can stop cursing!"

"Yes, I can speak the Word of God!"

"Yes, I can rejoice and be glad, even when I don't get my own way!"

"Yes, I can accept God's love for me and love Him back!"

"Yes, I can love myself!"

Life and power is in our wonderful One who loves us! We display self-control and courage when we take Him. It's rare that self-control exists without courage. J. Edgar Hoover once said, "I have never seen a courageous criminal." It takes courage to stop lying to yourself. Lying is rarely an isolated act. It becomes the servant of your abnormal acts. Be courageous and cut off your pursuit of lies by ending daydreaming, fictional dreams, and denial of the truth.

It takes self-control to deny yourself lustful imagining. You can take a diet pill to curb your appetite and you will lose weight, but if you were to gain godly peace in your soul by applying the truths I'm teaching you, you not only wouldn't need a diet pill but you also wouldn't need a diet to lose weight. Your mind would be filled with truth and love. You would not be vexed with strife, unhappiness, and discontent. Be sure to read my book *Free to Be Thin,* the Overeaters Victorious weight-loss method that works.

If you're going to change the circumstances around you, you have to change the thoughts within you. Complaining, daydreaming, wishing, lying, and envying other people

won't help you. These unbridled habits feed on themselves
and promote failure and despair.

Self-control pulls your mind out of destruction and shame
and into the love-mind and love-action heart of God.

Your mind is on Jesus, your King, the One who saves you
from yourself, from all destruction. Your God is not your
appetite. You do not wallow in shame, weeping, or self-destructive habits—you're free, you're His, and you're filled to
overflowing with new life and power from the Holy Spirit.

Believe.

Your self-control is the strongest link between you and
the exercise of your talents. You are the director of your
choices and the use of your talents. The next chapter will
talk about discovering your talent. You're a Loved Person
and you have talent, even if you don't think so.

test

it may not be the sweetest
flower to hold, the one
with thorns,
but you're stuck in a garden
where beauty comes with a price,
you feel like alice in wonderland
,it's all so strange
and you're wishing
you had stayed home with your old pals
sloth and
            laziness; you *enjoyed*
            your rebellion, you whimper,
like a cat,
but you know you must stay here
where it's hot, lonely,
self-denying, pAINful (at
times)
but you don't relent, you're committed
and you've said
        YES
to self-control

6

Possess and Use Your Talents

We want our lives to count for something. I receive many letters from people asking for help in finding value and purpose in their lives. I've prayed with and counseled countless men and women, young and old, from all walks of life, who have shared this deep and very real hunger for self-importance.

Tom Netherton, the television and concert singer, once told me, "All I ever wanted was my life to count for something."

When I wrote Tom's life story, *In the Morning of My Life,* it made me happy to see how God answered his fervent yearning for value in his life. I wrote about his search for self-worth and about how he finally found it.

Tom Netherton gave the Lord Jesus complete control of his life. It is when we lose ourselves to God that we become our true selves. This is true for you, for me, for every person who ever lived. I think Tom's life is a testimony to the faithfulness of God.

True success is entirely different from the world's interpretation of it. The same applies to talent.

A common mistake we make is equating talent with our personhood. To identify ourselves by our talents, or what we *do,* is a mistake. You are not what you *do.* If that were true, finding your self-worth would just be a matter of finding something you like to do, and doing it.

An artist I knew years ago had a note over his drawing board with a quote by George Bernard Shaw. It read, "If you keep busy enough doing the things you like to do, you won't have time to think about whether you're happy or not."

That doesn't sound like a very exciting way to live, does it? Jesus Christ doesn't give you a busy life to serve as a shot of novocaine to alleviate the pain. He gives you abundant life so that what you do resounds with the heartbeat of heaven, whether you're busy or not.

As a child I dreamed of being a ballerina. I studied ballet from the time I was about ten. By the time I was a teenager, I was dancing professionally with a ballet company. From there I went to New York to study acting and singing as well as dancing. I began landing parts in musicals and plays and my theatrical career was launched. Those years before I became totally committed to Christ were deceptive years. I was a Christian, all right, and I went to church, but my life revolved around one person only: me.

I thought of myself in terms of my talents. It was, "Hi, I'm Marie. I dance and sing and act. That's who I am." But that wasn't who I was.

The best thing in my life at the time was Marble Collegiate Church in New York City, where Norman Vincent Peale was the minister. I arrived at the services early and sat in the first pew. My hunger for God was insatiable. I'll never forget Dr. Peale leaning over the pulpit with his arms extended and saying in his wonderfully soft stage whisper, "Jesus Christ will give you the life you're looking for. *Take Him.*"

I decided to make Jesus the Lord of every audition, rehearsal, dance class, voice lesson, performance. But my personhood was still in my talents. Now it was, "Hi, I'm Marie. I dance and sing and act, and I do it all for Jesus."

But I didn't really know the heart of God. I could feel His presence and I knew He held the world as well as my life in His hand, but I thought of Him in terms of my own ambitions. My talents and I were one. I was still dancing, singing, acting Marie. There was no other me.

Later, when some of my poems were published and an art gallery accepted a couple of my paintings, I added some more labels of identification. I was now a poet and artist. My biggest asset was my energy. Running a close second was an insatiable curiosity and interest in things around me.

The deception was that I thought what a person *did* identified who they were. I saw what I *did* as my personhood and my life. My prayers were a constant flood of pleas to God for insight, strength, ability, and so on, for my *work*. I really saw myself only in terms of my work, my abilities, and creativity. If I prayed for others, it was for their creativity and work, too. Health, love, money, friends, and family were important, yes, but *really*, the most vital thing in life was art. I believed that and lived that.

But a person is more than what he or she does or accomplishes in art or any other field of endeavor. I respect you for *you*, not for what you do. As far as I'm concerned, you don't have to do anything great or be anything special to get my admiration. I'll always see in you something wonderful and beautiful. It's *you* who is special. What you do (go to school, run a store, tend a baby, drive a bus, paint pictures, write books, sing) is marvelous and worthy of praise, but the person you *are* is sublime.

Several years ago, one of my closest friends, a very talented actor, committed suicide. This shook me terribly. His talents hadn't been enough for him. Talent didn't make him happy. It didn't give him the peace, joy, or love he needed. His tal-

ent was a part of him, but not *all* of him. He was worth far
more than his talent. The people who loved him best missed
him after he died, missed the person. It was *he* who was valuable.

How many great artists and performers can you name
who are more famous for their personal problems than their
talent? Some performers like Edith Piaf, Billie Holiday,
Judy Garland, and Marilyn Monroe have combined personal unhappiness with talent and made them one. The
existential writers like Jean-Paul Sartre have made art
out of discontent and misery. Brilliantly talented artists
such as Vincent van Gogh, Henri Toulouse-Lautrec, and
Amedeo Modigliani lived for their art and died before their
time.

I remember when I was a young drama student in New
York at the Herbert Berghof School, my teacher, Uta
Hagen, told us, "You've got to know suffering if you want to
be a great artist." Famous composers who have given us the
most magnificent music ever written have died as madmen,
alone and sick. Was their ability to suffer included in their
genius? Where did their art and their personhood separate?
Jesus Christ helped me see the difference between my art
and the person I really am. As Christians, our definition
and understanding of suffering is not the same. We don't
wallow in suffering and accept it as our fate. Our personhood is not to be found in suffering, but in *conquering*. I discovered that Jesus Christ *Himself* is life. When I fell in love
with Him and dedicated my life to Him, my interest in myself died and a deep passion to serve and help other people
overcame me. I left New York and the bright lights for Chi-
cago, where I attended Bible college. My first book was
published in 1971, followed by ten more in the next ten
years. I taught speech and communication in a Bible school

in Minnesota from 1972–1975, and went to a secular university to receive a degree in psychology. After interning for three years I became a professional psychotherapist on staff in a clinic in Minnesota. I then continued in graduate school in California until completing my master's degree, and finally my doctorate, in psychology. As an author, teacher, and therapist, my life is totally different from my earlier plans.

It's amazing what can happen when the Lord gets hold of a life. Without being dedicated to Him, I could have lost out on the new life I found in Him as a people helper. I became the real me only after I gave myself totally to Him.

Love goes beyond talent. Talent can be controlled by pride, but love, never.

Love doesn't puff itself up. It doesn't seek its own. Pride, vanity, and talent may fail, but love never fails. The Loved Person lives with a permanent identity that isn't dependent upon skills, talents, or the ability to achieve.

The Loved Person's Real Talent

There's a wonderful story told by Jesus in the Book of Matthew, chapter 25, that relates directly to you and me right now. The Jerusalem Bible says it this way:

> "[The kingdom of heaven will be like] a man on his way abroad who summoned his servants and entrusted his property to them. To one he gave five talents, to another two, to a third one; each in proportion to his ability. Then he set out. The man who had received the five talents promptly went and traded with them and made five more. The man who had received two made two more in the same way. But the man who had received one went off and dug a hole in the ground and hid his master's money. Now a long time after, the master of those servants came back and went

through his accounts with them. The man who had received the five talents came forward bringing five more. 'Sir,' he said, 'you entrusted me with five talents; here are five more that I have made.' His master said to him, 'Well done, good and faithful servant; you have shown you can be faithful in small things, I will trust you with greater; come and join in your master's happiness.' Next the man with the two talents came forward. 'Sir,' he said, 'you entrusted me with two talents; here are two more that I have made.' His master said to him, 'Well done, good and faithful servant; you have shown you can be faithful in small things, I will trust you with greater; come and join in your master's happiness.' Last came forward the man who had one talent. 'Sir,' said he, 'I had heard you were a hard man, reaping where you have not sown and gathering where you have not scattered; so I was afraid, and I went off and hid your talent in the ground. Here it is; it was yours, you have it back.' But his master answered him, 'You wicked and lazy servant! So you knew that I reap where I have not sown and gather where I have not scattered? Well then, you should have deposited my money with the bankers, and on my return I would have recovered my capital with interest. So now, take the talent from him and give it to the man who has the five talents. For to everyone who has will be given more, and he will have more than enough; but from the man who has not, even what he has will be taken away. As for this good-for-nothing servant, throw him out into the dark, where there will be weeping and grinding of teeth.' "

Matthew 25:14–30

I want you to see the servants in this story as representing you and me. The master in the story entrusted his servants with something precious and important to all concerned. We are the Christians in God's household. Our Master is the Lord Jesus Christ.

The Lord entrusts you and me with His Holy Spirit.

Without this certain Talent, we can do nothing. God's heart of love brooding over His creation, the knowledge that "the earth is the Lord's, and the fulness thereof; the world, and they that dwell therein" (Psalms 24:1), and the power to do His will would be as still as a body with no breath without this Talent. Our Talent is the Holy Spirit and I want to show you, through this parable, some things that may revolutionize your life, as they have mine.

The master gave his servants money (a talent was worth about one thousand dollars). Jesus gives you and me something far more precious—His Holy Spirit.

> Your talent is not singing or dancing or cooking or race-car driving or growing flowers or playing the bassoon or flying airplanes or anything of the sort—your Talent is the Holy Spirit.

The three servants received their talents according to how much they were able to manage. The servant who received only one talent was weak and the master knew it. That's why he didn't entrust him with more. The Bible says, "The just shall live by faith," and this servant must have lacked faith. In spite of this, his master's heart of love entrusted him with a talent.

Love, you see, hopes all things. "Let the weak say, I am strong," the Bible tells us, so we are never without hope. Nobody is ever *too* weak. He can strengthen our faith. God told us the weak can say, "I'm strong!" because He provided His strength for ours.

His gift to you is Himself: His mind, heart, and ability. This you have through the Person of the Holy Spirit.

In verse 16 of Matthew 25, the first servant takes his five talents and immediately figures out a way to increase them.

He represents the Christian who takes the Holy Spirit without fear or reservation, and by manifesting the gifts and fruit of the Holy Spirit in his life, he is ready for more.

As a Christian person who is acutely conscious of the love you're loved with, you can dare to take the gift He has given you and allow it to multiply within you. The Holy Spirit will produce more of Himself in your life and the result is, He increases and you decrease. Your human nature takes on His *divine* nature.

Which Servant Are You?

Think of Jesus Christ as the Master of your house. If those servants had respected their master's wishes, all *three* would have multiplied what he gave them. Which of the servants represents you?

The servant who buried his talent is like the Christian who tries to buy the Holy Spirit. This person digs a hole for his Talent by arguing and fighting with God's Word. "Do not quench (suppress or subdue) the (Holy) Spirit," we read in 1 Thessalonians 5:19 (AMPLIFIED). The Lord tells us to be happy in our faith, rejoicing and being glad-hearted continually. We dig the hole deeper when we refuse. We lie to ourselves with words like, "Life is just a series of ups and downs. Nothing good lasts. I'm just a burnt-out charcoal in the great barbecue of life!"

The servant who buried his talent accused his master of being a "hard man." He accused him of not being loving! If that wasn't bad enough, he handed the talent right back to his master. A gift from God is precious and is meant to be multiplied. To throw it back in His face unused is unthinkable.

The lazy, wicked servant committed a gross injustice to

his master by giving back an unused and unexercised talent. It was such a malodorous insult that the master was infuriated beyond entreaty. Compare his situation with ours. We receive the Talent of the Holy Spirit, who is the Lifegiver. *It is the Spirit who gives life* (John 6:63). It stands to reason that if we refuse to take life, we die.

To make matters worse, the wicked servant made excuses for his sin, which showed his unregenerate and unrepentant heart. A sign of blasphemy against the Holy Spirit is the inability to repent. You reap what you sow. Refusing Jesus Christ, who lives in you by His Holy Spirit, burying Him, and throwing Him back at the face of God with diatribes about His being mean and unjust, is refusing life.

You cannot impress God with your human abilities. He knows all about what you can and can't do in your own strength. If you want to make a real imprint on this world, do something great in life, count yourself as worthwhile, use your Talent.

Put aside those aspirations that vaunt your own natural abilities over the power of God in your life (including in your ministry). Almost everyone has some sort of natural talent. God wants *you.*

The reward for the two servants who used their talents is what every person on earth wants: joy, delight, blessedness: "... Enter into and share the joy—the delight, the blessedness—which your master [enjoys]" (Matthew 25:23 AMPLIFIED).

The investment of the Holy Spirit in a human life has incomparable rewards. The master told the servants who invested wisely, "Well done, good and faithful servant; you have shown you can be faithful in small things, I will trust you with greater...."

How do you apply the truths in this parable to your life? Let me give you a progression to bring you to the point where you will unquestionably "enter into the joy of the Lord."

How to possess and use your talent:

1. Receive the Talent, which is the Holy Spirit within you.
2. Exercise the Talent so He will multiply within you. This is done by believing in Him and who He is through faithful meditating (walking and talking) the Word of God.
3. Give yourself as a gift to God. You're a Spirit-filled, Spirit-multiplied person and you belong to Him. He promises to enter you into His joy.
4. Receive your interests, skills, fruitful endeavors, labors, and works. (Here's where you can develop your dream of skydiving for Jesus or heavenly hairdressing or writing, singing, cooking, mule packing—whatever!) Because He has found you faithful in a little, He can give you much.
5. Now because your main Talent and lifeline is the power of the Holy Spirit, all that you do you do with the joy of the Lord as your strength. Though things get rough and you find yourself in difficult straits, you have entered into the Master's joy and you don't quit or despair.
6. You continue to multiply and multiply. "For to everyone who has will be given more, and he will have more than enough."
7. He gives unto you good measure, running over for the purpose of your giving to others. You're now able to obey the Holy Spirit as He moves you into the realm of the Lord's New Commandment. "Then shall the righteous shine forth as the sun in the kingdom of their Father ..." (Matthew 13:43).

You're shining with a dazzling light of power and love, multiplying the power of the Holy Spirit within you and through you.

Now you're *really* Talented.

at a gallery

Painted figurines
                standing in a row
,all exactly alike
                and
                lifeless;
        no magician-beautician
                could
                engineer
                them into
                joy
                        or (even
)
                        apathy
        ;and there
                a robust sculpture
        bearing the integrity
                of a century
                        ,paintings
                        splendid with
                        inventiveness
                                style&skill
        but
                Jesus
                loves
                the
                artist
                more
                than
                art.

7

How to Be a Lover

When I immersed myself in God's love and thoroughly realized that I was a Loved Person, I wanted to start living it. I asked myself a question. It was a crucial question, one I thought about very seriously and still do: "Now that I *know* I'm loved and valuable, how do I treat others? *Can I accept others unconditionally?*"

Let me tell you a true story. There was a young girl of about nineteen who quit smoking after she dedicated her life to Jesus. She was delighted with herself. She hadn't smoked for nearly a year, when one day she bought a package of cigarettes for "just one little puff." Before long, her habit was in full swing again. Her mother came to visit, and they were sitting in the living room in chairs opposite each other. The girl took out her cigarettes, lit one, and smoked it. Later, as she and her mother were sitting there chatting, the girl lamented, "I feel so bad that I started smoking again."

The mother looked at her startled. "*What?* You started smoking again? When?" She hadn't even noticed her daughter light up the cigarette and puff away on it. She hadn't even smelled the smoke. She didn't see it because she didn't expect it. She wasn't on the lookout for her daughter to make mistakes or hurt herself.

When our hearts are set on loving each other, we don't look for mistakes or hurts: we look to love.

Love is always on the lookout to give itself. Love pulses with burgeoning cravings to explode on others. It is not my goal with this book to point a bony finger at the sins of the world. It is rather to usher in the wealth of joy, beauty, and glory in the love of Jesus. If you see His love and take it, the sin will fall from you like the peeling off a banana. The girl in this story was me.

Water can't quench the fire of God's love for His own beloved ones. Nothing can. Selfish love, on the other hand, alienates and offends, and is constantly burned-out like withered, scorched grass. It hungrily seeks to fulfill itself and never does.

It's necessary to make a distinction between self-love, or autoerotism, and the passions of our beloved Loved Person, who is *you,* hero emeritus of this book. Narcissism is abnormal self-love. It insults true love, because true love is selfless.

I once counseled a lovely couple who were having trouble in their marriage. I saw them individually and then together. When they were alone with me, they were each charming, sweet, and gentle, but together they became uncontrollably hostile. Once the wife picked up something from my desk and threw it at her husband. He clenched his fist and shouted at the top of his voice. That session was quite lively, to say the least.

Self-love was destroying them. Each of them was fighting for something they called "rights." Each demanded that the other acquiesce to his or her wants and desires. They had preconceived ideas about marriage and neither of them was matching up to what the other expected.

"He sleeps late. He doesn't pick up after himself. He doesn't help with the kids. He's lazy and unambitious. I can't stand it."

"She's cold, nasty. She finds fault with everything I do. She's trying to run my life. I can't stand it."

"He said—"

"She said—"

"He won't fulfill my expectations."

"She won't fulfill my demands."

"It's terrible."

"It's awful."

"She's supposed to make me happy."

"He's supposed to make *me* happy."

As I counseled this couple I could see that their expectations far outweighed their ability to perform. They were swept away with frustration and disappointment. Their marriage was like being in a boat grounded on rocks in the shallow waters of selfish love: as long as it remains tied up in those shallow waters, it will never do what a boat is meant to do—sail. When the boat does launch out into the deep, where mutual respect and common decency are necessary at the helm, that boat capsizes.

"I'm bailing out," says one.

"This boat is not for me," says the other.

"Sea life is not what I thought it would be."

"It's all *your* fault. You're a rotten sailor."

Someone once said, "If you can't love your enemies, at least be kind to your friends." I would like to suggest husbands and wives be friends. G. K. Chesterton said, "A man's friend *likes* him but leaves him as he is; his wife *loves* him and is always trying to turn him into somebody else." Husbands do the same to wives.

Often we are kinder to strangers than to people we know and care about. The axiom "You always hurt the one you love" is a callow excuse and tells us that love needs improvement if it's going to continue to be called love.

When I think of love, I think of acceptance. When people tell me they love me, I hope they're telling me they accept me, and that, in their opinion, I'm okay as I am.

Where Are Your Rights?

Connie says all men are rotten chauvinists. She says all a man wants is for a woman to do his dirty work, provide him with sex, and give him babies (but not too many). I met Connie one summer while my daughters and I were wilderness camping. She had pitched her tent about a quarter of a mile from ours; she was all alone. I passed her while hauling water back to our campsite and I felt compassion for her, thinking she might be out there sorting out her thoughts after a divorce or a death in the family. She looked so desolate. Wilderness camping alone, I thought, couldn't be that much of a treat. At home there was the dishwasher, the microwave oven, and hot water, but out there beneath the stars it was Coleman burners and a water pump two miles away.

I was surprised to learn that the brave camper was vindictively proving to her "chauvinist" husband that she could do something on her own. She became enraged later on that night when he showed up with their three strapping teenage boys for a wienie roast. Since we had a fire already going, they roasted their hot dogs at our campsite.

Connie's husband argued with her, insisting she should come home where it was warm, and besides, there were good shows on TV that night. Connie wasn't about to budge. After her husband and sons left, she told me angrily, "He wants me to cook something or clean something. He doesn't even know where the eggs are in the refrigerator, and he hasn't picked up a dust cloth in twenty-two years of marriage."

Where were her *rights?* she wanted to know. "When do I do something for *me?*" She didn't realize there is a way to communicate one's wants successfully. There is a way to let your feelings be known without heading for the wilderness to battle it out alone with the mosquitoes and the Coleman burners, only to return home to find the situation exactly the same—except dustier.

Suppose Connie had gone home and sat down with her husband and said something like this: "I have decided to free you from the demands I have made on you all these years."

Her husband would no doubt be startled by such words. "Demands? What demands?"

"In the past I have demanded that you be responsible for my happiness and my fulfillment as a human being."

"Huh?"

"I'm going to love you and cherish you, but I am going to find my personhood in the Lord Jesus."

"Huh?"

"I am going to reach out to life and embrace it. If I am unhappy with something, I am going to express it, but not for the purpose of getting my own way."

"Am I hearing right?"

"Yes, I've decided not to manipulate to get my own way. I am going to state my wants clearly and directly, for you to accept or not to accept."

"Well, I never—"

"Furthermore, I am going to give you the right to make mistakes. I can do that because I first am giving myself the right to make mistakes."

"That's nice. For supper I want eggs."

It will take Connie and her husband time to learn how to live a life of honest and direct communicating. By honest I do not mean hurtful. Don't think you're being honest when you say something like, "You big jerk! You make me sick."

An honest statement would be, "I'm concerned about such-and-such and I'd like to talk to you about it, because I care about you and I know you care about me." Make it an "I" message instead of a "you" accusation.

Lovers Are Guilt Free

A lover doesn't condemn the one he loves.

You can't hand out condemnation and love at the same time. You may frequently condemn yourself and others, *blaming* them, yourself, or even fate for being cruel, unfair or unkind, but as a lover you are free from condemnation. The way to stop irrational condemning is first to see that *you* are magnificently prized by God. Then, second, realize He took all the blame for those injustices you're upset about.

When you blame yourself or others, you get angry and hostile. When these emotions are turned inward, you become depressed. But why the blame in the first place? The anger you feel says so-and-so is to blame for your hurt; that's why you're upset. You're saying, (1) I don't like so-and-so's behavior. (2) Because I don't like it, he or she shouldn't do it. In other words, you're the boss, the judge. Even if you're right about so-and-so's behavior, your condemning will probably not help to stop it. To quote Dr. Albert Ellis: "Blame or guilt, instead of alleviating wrong-doing, often leads to further immorality, hypocrisy, and evasion of responsibility."

Condemn a person and you alienate the person. One couple who came to see me for marriage counseling complained acidly of each other's faults:

"He took me away from a wonderful life in Walla Walla."

"She never sticks up for me."

"He makes stupid mistakes."

"She insists on going to work when she knows I hate it."

"He's an idiot."

"She's a shrew."

Each of them *blamed* the other, and did it do any good?

"Do you both feel better about each other after saying the things you just said?" I asked.

"Heavens, no. Why should we?"

This conversation is typical. One spouse accuses and blames. The other strikes a main line of defense. Common protection against condemnation is to condemn back.

You can accept or discard blame or condemnation that is placed upon you. If you accept blame, you'll defend yourself, fight back, attack, condemn in return. Discard it, refuse it, and you're free. Somebody once said, "Refuse a gift and it remains with its donor." Even if you have done wrong, ask for forgiveness and then leave the condemnation in the gutter where it comes from and where it belongs.

It is a wrong notion that we *should* blame ourselves and condemn ourselves for every wrongdoing. Your friends, relatives, and acquaintances may insist upon it, but you do not have to agree with this hypothesis. Because you make a mistake does not mean you are a worthless human being and deserve condemnation.

The husband in the couple I was counseling had feelings of worthlessness, because he (mis)believed that his wife's diatribes were legitimate. He attacked in return, because he felt justified in blaming her for his unhappiness.

This couple's prolific use of energy defeated their hopes for happiness. I tried to point out to them that condemnation is a choice. It is vital to know what the Lord is saying about you. You have given Him your life and you are a

Christian bearing the banner of *beauty*. God does not jump down your throat when you make a mistake. He brought you to His banquet hall for the purpose of loving you and making you like Himself. His banner over you is love. I like this quotation by Horace Greeley. "I am the inferior of any man whose rights I trample underfoot." Don't trample your own right to joy by condemning yourself. "He that believeth on him is not condemned . . ." (John 3:18).

Listen to Romans 8:1 (AMPLIFIED) and absorb it into your heart: "Therefore [there is] now no condemnation—no adjudging guilty of wrong—for those who are in Christ Jesus, who live not after the dictates of the flesh, but after the dictates of the Spirit."

You are a Loved Person. You're not to be condemned or snared by the crooked behaviors of pride and self-defense. You can say, with the Apostle Paul, "For I know that nothing good dwells within me, that is, in my flesh . . ." (Romans 7:18 AMPLIFIED), and you can further celebrate, "I endorse and delight in the Law of God in my inmost self—with my new nature" (Romans 7:22 AMPLIFIED).

Stop Condemning Yourself

What can you do to change your blaming, condemning behaviors?

1. When you feel guilty and condemned by your own mistakes, examine what you're telling yourself. The words you tell yourself create your self-condemnation. You will say, (a) "I did a rotten job of [blank] concluding that (b) I am a rotten person." This, of course, is utter fiction. You can change these words to: (a) "Though I did wrong, (b) it is something humans frequently do—even born-again, Spirit-filled Christians sometimes make mistakes, and (c) I can, with the help of the Lord, improve my behavior."

I have the right to make mistakes. To make a mistake is human. To forgive is godly.

2. Realize changing takes work. If you wanted to be an expert glassblower, you'd have to train, practice, and learn the art of glassblowing. If you want to be an expert at being you, you have to train for it and work at it. If you want to be free of condemnation in your life, you will have to combat the lies you tell yourself. John Knox said, "I thank God that I have come in the thick of the battle." Jesus is in the thick of your battle. He is ready to stand at your side and battle those self-sabotaging falsehoods that can suck the joy out of you and sap you of beauty and strength.

3. Learn to distinguish between condemnation and responsibility. You are responsible for your own behavior but because you behaved in a less-than-perfect way does not mean you are a worthless person. You are responsible for your own attitude toward others, too. Because they perform in a less-than-perfect way does not make them worthless persons.

4. Realize that because *you* don't like something or what somebody does, he or she is not necessarily wrong. Your likes and dislikes have nothing whatever to do with right and wrong. I know a man who hates tennis. He has a son who plays every day. The father fumes in disapproval because he misbelieves that his own personal likes and dislikes dictate right and wrong for others. In his opinion, the son is wasting his time.

You'd be surprised if you knew how often we condemn others because of our own personal likes and dislikes. We might say, "Can you believe the loud and tacky clothes that woman has the nerve to wear?" (In other words, she's *wrong* to do such a thing because I don't like it.)

"It just burns me up the way some people spend their time." (In other words, I'm the one with the authority to say what is worthwhile and what isn't. If people don't meet my expectations, they're wrong.)

"How can you eat that awful-looking stuff?" (Because I don't like it, you shouldn't, either.)

"I can't stand the way so-and-so throws away his money on his stupid hobbies." (I'm the one who says what's stupid and what isn't. If I don't like it, it's stupid.)

"The way so-and-so [pastor, group leader, mayor, president] runs things is terrible." (I don't like it so it's terrible. People should do things the way I want them to. If they don't, they're wrong.)

It is acceptable to dislike the behaviors of others as well as your own, but you need not be a victim of them. You can constructively learn to change and help others to change by discarding condemnation and blaming from your life. Dr. Albert Ellis tells his clients:

> You may choose to climb the highest available mountain for several good reasons. You may, for example, enjoy climbing; delight in the challenge this difficult peak presents; or want to thrill to the view from the top. But you also may have bad reasons for climbing the same mountain; to look down and spit at the people below.

You're not a spitter, you're a lover. Love will make you what your heart has craved, and you won't feel guilty when you get there.

i promise guiltless

because
i love you
for you,
i allow you
the right
to be the you
you want to be.
　　i will not demand that
　　you
　　　　do as i say
　　　　be as i say
and i promise not to drop
the weight of my life and needs
on the hollow of your back.
i want to love God more
　　and love you more,
　　　　too,
deeper, better, sweeter, and yes,
　　　　true and now,
　　i promise i will never
　　　　　　never
sic on you the snapping, snarling
　　　　　　hounds of
guilt

Part II

Living in Love

How do we *live* love? How do we dedicate ourselves to being Loved Persons and *living* in love? Sometimes it takes a while to become the expressions of love we are called to be. I think of Saint Francis who, after being called by God to rebuild the church, spent an entire year in prayer, seeking God's will. Then it took several months more of prayer before God guided him into a mighty ministry which became one of the most celebrated the world has ever known.

One day as Francis returned from the caves of Mount Subasio, where he prayed every day, he heard the ominous bell of an approaching leper. He recoiled because he couldn't stand the sight of a leper. In the past he had become ill at the sight of one. As the leper approached, Francis looked at his horribly deformed face and said, ". . . thousands of people, and each one of them is unique."

It was a thought too beautiful to have been his own. He embraced the leper and apologized for his previous attitude. He thought it strange, as he held the horrible creature in his arms, that he did not reek of the awful leper stench of illness and decay. He gave him the money in his pocket and then the leper vanished. When Francis breathed again, the air had suddenly become sweet and pure.

"Inasmuch as ye have done it unto one of the least of these my brethren, ye have done it unto me" (Matthew 25:40). Would you say Saint Francis had learned how to live in love?

This section of the book is lovingly dedicated to your everyday life. I believe in you and in your incredible potential to live in love as a Loved Person. Starting with yourself, being a Loved Person is an everyday experience. Knowing how loved you are is the first step into your new life. *Living* it is the next.

You can bring sweetness where there was sorrow, joy where there was agony. Saint Francis lived in the thirteenth century, but you live now. Living in love is now. It's for you.

8

Never Say Fail

If you could hear the audible voice of God each day, what do you suppose you'd hear Him say? Would you hear, "Good morning, My darling Christian person! I love you!" Or would He grumble, "Wake up, dumb head, it's time for you to realize again what a total loser you are!"

Do you suppose the Lord speaks to His family with curses or with blessings? Does He look at you with tenderness and love, or does He snarl and snap at you with put-downs night and day? Which is it? You've got to know.

Jesus said, "My sheep hear my voice, and I know them, and they follow me" (John 10:27). If you believe in God and His Son, Jesus Christ, if you call yourself a Christian, then Jesus, your Savior, says you can hear His voice. You have the ability to hear Him. What is He saying to you?

My dear, you're hearing a *wrong* voice if you aren't hearing Him tell you what He has already said about you in the Bible. If you believe you're a failure, a wreck of a human being, a nothing, you're hearing the wrong voice.

Humility is never self-destroying. It's self-understanding. Just imagine the Lord Jesus Christ, our perfectly humble Savior, telling His disciples, "I feel like such a total dud as I stand here today. I am the way, the truth, and the life."

One of the most common self-put-downs I hear is, "I'm a failure." Another is, "What if I fail?" Still another, "I'm

97

afraid I'll fail"—failure-centered self-talk. Everything on earth can fall to shreds, but love does not fail. God is love. God doesn't fail. Jesus knew that.

Failure, thoughts of failure, and fear of it have no place in your loved life anymore. Failure may have once been something you dreaded; in fact, you may have lived your life trying to avoid it. Your friends, pursuits, plans, business and personal dealings might have been wrapped up in your overwhelming fear of failure. But now you're energized by the love of God. Your life is a loved life, filled with the understanding of who you are and what you request.

No weapon formed against you shall prosper (Isaiah 54:17), and you can believe it. In the morning when you awaken, tell yourself, "I am like a tree planted by rivers of water and whatsoever I do shall prosper [*see* Psalms 1:3] and *I don't fail!*"

What Is Failure?

What do you interpret as failure? Here is a man who laments, "I tuned the car myself, and it broke down after twenty-five miles, so I had it towed to a service station where I filled the tank with gas and forgot to put the cap back on the gas tank. Then when I parked and locked up, I looked in the window and saw the keys were still in the ignition. I'm a failure at everything I do."

A middle-aged woman complains that no matter how hard she works, other people always reap better rewards. She has been at the same job for ten years and yet a friend who joined the company two short years ago just received a huge promotion and raise.

"I never get any breaks," she grumbles bitterly. "Nothing goes right for me. I bought a coat the other day for a hundred dollars. I thought it was such a bargain. Two days later the same coat went on sale for fifty dollars. I'm a failure at everything I do."

What is failure? What is success?

Here's another person with problems that seem unsurmountable, too. He lost his job because the company he worked for went out of business. His friends worry whether he will lose his faith in the Lord now that he has no job and no income. But he rises to the occasion and tells them, "I'm not happy about losing my job, and I'm tempted to be downright upset about it, but I'm going to believe what the Word of God says instead of my own emotions."

We could call this man "Mr. Loved Person." He quotes the Word of God, which says that God will supply all his needs according to His riches in glory by Christ Jesus (Philippians 4:19). He says, "I choose to believe that with the Lord as my Shepherd, I shall not want!" He is willing to start afresh with renewed hope. He sees himself as precious to God.

Mr. Loved Person has other problems on his mind, too. He has an alcoholic sister for whom he has prayed for almost sixteen years. His sister's condition is getting worse instead of better. She seems to be going further away from God instead of drawing closer. His friends at church tell him that his sister may just be hopeless, and there's nothing he can do about it. They tell him his financial situation is just bad luck.

You must realize your prayers are precious to God. He knows and hears and answers. You must see that God's purpose is to redeem and to deliver people from defeat and despair. As a Loved Person you insist upon seeing God's will accomplished. You remain on the battlefield for others, as the brother of the alcoholic sister does. He doesn't pray with fear or doubt in his heart. He *knows* the Lord Jesus has defeated the works of the devil, and he *knows* his authority as God's child. He does not lose heart or weary of well-doing. He knows the effectual, fervent prayer of a righteous man or woman avails much. He knows the heart of God and he will not give up.

It's like the man whose barn burned down. He could have used the situation to become bitter, angry, or upset with God. Instead, he looked out over the charred ruins from his porch and exclaimed, "Praise the Lord, now I can see the moon."

Because you're a Loved Person and love is patient, you are patient. Love is steadfast so you are steadfast. You're not a chump "rolling with the punches," you're a fighter fighting for God's success in your life.

Make these choices:

- I will not talk failure talk.
- I will not think failure thoughts.
- I will see myself as a success because that's how God sees me.
- In Jesus' name, I refuse to fail.
- In Jesus' name, I *am* a success.

If you define failure as something that happens to you or something you make happen, you're mistaken. If you define your personal success as something you do outside of God's control, something you achieve by your own acumen and prowess, you're mistaken. What you believe about yourself is shadowed with wrong thinking and misbelief. It's not what success and failure are all about.

The high-school student says, "I'm a success because I got an *A* on the exam." The car salesman says, "I'm a success because I sold three cars today." The housewife says, "I'm a success because I've been married to the same man for ten years."

What happens when the student gets a *C* on the next exam, when the car salesman doesn't sell any cars for three months, and when the housewife receives a packet containing divorce papers?

I thought I was the most wonderful wife who ever boiled an egg or swept the porch. I *believed* in myself as a wife. After all, I adored my husband, sacrificed for him, stood by him through thick and thin. My whole world was wrapped up in him. If someone asked me, "How are you, Marie?" I told them about my husband. I learned through him how deeply I could care. I tried to make his needs and wants more important than my own. Aren't these the things that make a happy husband?

When our children were born and I saw what beautiful little people they were, I thought surely I had everything a girl could want. We didn't have much money, but we had a wonderful family and love, I told myself.

My husband left me and found himself another woman. It was a complete shock to me. I thought I had a happy marriage. One day I might even have taught or written about how to be a wonderful wife. Imagine! I might have taught somebody that success is something you *do*, meaning you're good at something, and that love is something you *earn*. I might have taught people that happiness is finding yourself and your personhood in another human being, as I had once believed. I was so wrong.

Another person mustn't hold the strings of your personhood. Our personhood is to be found in Jesus Christ. We are a success because He is a success. We live and breathe suc-

cess. Even though we may be rejected, or we may lose something precious to us, we are winners. The Christian is not a
failure.

We may feel like failures from time to time. I was devas-
tated by my husband's rejection. Certainly I felt I was a failure. After waiting for three years for him to return, I realized he wasn't going to, and we were divorced. I thought I
had been a good wife, giving my best. I was able to ask
God's forgiveness for the pride that refused to see my own
faults and shortcomings. I had a long season of repentance
and finally, I began to come out of the doldrums of despair
and shame. It wasn't easy, though. My self-image was less
than nothing. I felt like a dirty rug in the great doorway of
life.

Jesus was wounded and hung on the cross so that we
could succeed with Him, even when it looks as though we
are total failures. He triumphed over failure and death. He
redeemed us from the curse of the law and made us winners
in spite of ourselves. I allowed Him the right to change me,
heal me, and best of all—to love me.

God understands how we feel when we're rejected. Jesus
gave His best when He lived on earth. He healed the sick,
raised the dead, made the blind to see and the lame to walk.
He brought the Word of truth and love to the world. He
gave His best. And what happened? He was rejected and
despised.

Do you believe that success is something you *do* by your
own efforts? Is success something somebody else defines for
you?

Success is Jesus Christ. Because you are filled with the
Holy Spirit of God, walking and moving on the face of
this earth in His Power and love, *you are a success.*

If you think of yourself as a person who fails, you'll talk and behave accordingly. I realize that even though I failed as a wife in someone else's eyes, I am not a failure. Though I lost a way of life and the love of a person, I am not a loser and I am not unlovable. Though I am faced with a singularity I do not choose or want, I am not helpless or hopeless. Success is in Jesus.

Love Thoughts for Success

Teach yourself to think the way the Lord thinks, especially when you seem to fail. He is giving you new thoughts—His thoughts.

Say out loud:

- I am a Loved Person. I am precious to God. I do not judge my success or failure on how well I perform a task or skill.
- I am a Loved Person. I am precious to God. I am not a success or failure because I do or do not meet somebody else's expectations of me.
- I am a Loved Person. I am precious to God. I reject the non-Christian interpretation of success and failure.
- I am a Loved Person. I am precious to God. Because He is a success, I am, too. I am changed into His image by the Holy Spirit.
- I am a Loved Person. I am precious to God. I cannot fail because I no longer live by my own might or my own power, but by the Holy Spirit.
- I am a Loved Person. I am precious to God. I choose not to be conformed to this world, but to live in the love of Christ, which passes knowledge. I am filled with the fullness of God.
- I am a Loved Person. I am precious to God. I will not be afraid of success, nor will I stand in its way in my life. Success will neither destroy nor hurt me because my success is of God. The Lord is on my side!

I wrote a book about a man who was sold as a slave when he was just five years old (*Help Me Remember ... Help Me Forget* [formerly *The Emancipation of Robert Sadler*]). He lived as a slave on a cotton plantation and he suffered a miserable life of deprivation, humiliation, pain, and fear. He was treated as something less than human. But Robert Sadler became one of the most vibrant, loving ministers of the Gospel of Christ I have ever known.

He radiated with love. Wherever he went, people were drawn to him. I've seen people burst into tears as he sang or spoke, utterly convicted of their sin and humbled before God. Early one morning we stood on a train platform in Ohio: Robert Sadler, my two little girls, and I. We had been working on and researching his book, and now I was returning to my home to write. A man approached us and began chatting, and Robert Sadler asked him if he knew Jesus Christ as his Lord.

The man said, "I don't go for that religious stuff. I'm seventy-two years young and, knock wood, still going strong."

Robert Sadler shook his head sadly and said, "You mean, you've lived for seventy-two years and you *still* don't know enough to make Jesus Christ your Lord?"

It wasn't too long before the man was in tears. Robert Sadler's gentle voice of love, his warmth, and genuine godly heart were too much for the man to resist. He gave his heart to the Lord right there.

To some people, being sold as a slave would mean failure, a terrible tragedy. Certainly you don't equate slavery with the bittersweet smell of worldly success. But because of the power of the Holy Spirit, Sadler rose above circumstances and triumphed in the eyes of all heaven. His life made an impact on countless thousands of lives. He was a man of love and power. In my opinion, he was a total success.

What is success? Isn't it living the life Jesus would live if He were here now? Isn't it hearing the voice of the Holy Spirit gently guiding you and teaching you all things?

Overcoming and persevering is what success is all about. And the highest plateau of success is to persevere with loving patience and to overcome life's hurdles joyfully. To experience a trial without despair, and to suffer loss without bitterness, to fight for the blessings that are ours and count it all joy—that's success.

It's time to evaluate our thoughts of success. If God doesn't look at you and see Jesus, you're not a success. You may be on the road to it, persevering and overcoming in Christ, but without joy, peace, and *love,* you're not there yet. Jesus is the success, remember. It's through *Him* you succeed. You and I were born to live totally in Him; to fulfill the Word which reads, "I am crucified with Christ: nevertheless I live; yet not I, but Christ liveth in me: and the life which I now live in the flesh I live by the faith of the Son of God, who loved me, and gave himself for me" (Galatians 2:20).

That's success.

punching at love

There's punching
trouble, anger;
        a bubble
of fury
,all in a hurry
—surely
you don't mean
that miserable scene
     ;that fit of screaming
     ;you must be dreaming.
Nice people don't curse
     ,there's nothing worse

than
a human full of
    human
    weakness
            ,is that how you feel?
(i thought so.)

            Oh, but
            there's
            sweetness, delightful
                    meat of the fruit
            ,luscious
                    ,a good aftertaste
            ,a lingering
                goodness
                    because a human
                            full of
                    human weakness
            makes for the most free
                        (forever-ly)
            lamb of the Lord God

and that's what you are
                ,free
eating of the sweetmeats
        of God
        in Christ
and no matter how often
            you punch at love
there will never be
                a fist
                from above
punching
        you
        back

9

How to Stop Being Afraid

The first time I was in Europe was in 1977 while researching my book *Of Whom the World Was Not Worthy.* I had traveled through Yugoslavia from Slovenia to Macedonia, interviewing peasants, gypsies, factory workers, doctors, and laborers, as well as ex-officials of the Communist party. I wanted to know how the Christians' faith was sustained through the devastating years of World Wars I and II. I learned that they had simply clung to God with an almost incredible faith.

It had been a fruitful journey so far, and I was excited about this final lap from Eastern through Western Europe. I was somewhat fearful, however, and nervous about how to get along with so many people, languages, and places. The Lord spoke to my heart when I was searching for a restaurant in Vienna. I didn't know where to go, but I was following directions to a place recommended in my tourist's guidebook. It was getting late and I was growing tired and frustrated. It was then God spoke to me. He said, *Marie, no matter what you do, do nothing out of fear.*

I will never forget those words. *No matter what you do, do nothing out of fear.* A sudden energy rushed through my entire being. My shyness and inhibitions seemed ridiculous. I felt renewed, confident, and unafraid. It just didn't make sense to be afraid!

How do you stop being afraid? How do you cast out fear so that love may rule and reign in your life?

I'd like you to do something with me right now. Are you willing? Right now, take a deep breath, relax, and concentrate on what I'm about to tell you.

Here it is: imagine the Lord Jesus Christ standing beside you right where you are now. He is close enough to touch. Imagine yourself looking up at Him, into His sweet, beautiful face, filled with compassion.

Imagine Him putting His arms around you and holding you as an eagle hides her young in the warmth of her feathers. Think of yourself as hidden in Him—hidden in His presence and His love for you. He is all love. His presence is love. His words are love. His actions are love.

He loves you.

Now He is talking to you. His voice is soft at first. You aren't even sure if it *is* a voice. It's so gentle. There is no tension in that voice, no anxiety. It's a pure sound, unworldly, unfamiliar. Its sound is utter peace, incredibly still and small. Yet it also is the sound of mighty, rushing waters. Be very quiet now.

Listen, He speaks directly to you:

> Fear not; [there is nothing to fear] for I am with you; do not look around you in terror and be dismayed, for I am your God. I will strengthen and harden you [to difficulties]; yes, I will help you; yes, I will hold you up and retain you with My victorious right hand of rightness and justice.
>
> Isaiah 41:10 AMPLIFIED

Listen again. "Fear not; there is nothing to fear."

He smiles at you. His countenance is dazzling and all-encompassing. How He loves you. His attention is directly upon you. He came to see only you, to speak to only you.

There is no crowd around you. You are alone with Him. "For I, the Lord your God, hold your right hand; I, Who say to you, Fear not, I will help you!" (Isaiah 41:13 AMPLIFIED). Now repeat the words He has spoken to you:

> I will fear not. There is nothing to fear because He is with me. I will not look around in terror and be dismayed, for He is my God. He strengthens and hardens me to difficulties. He helps me. He holds me up and keeps me with His victorious right hand of rightness and justice.

His words are like warm waters around you. They are truth and they are life. He says your name. "Fear not: for I have redeemed thee, I have called thee by thy name; thou art mine" (Isaiah 43:1).

Let His words soak into your mind and your heart. Respond to them. I'm sharing this understanding with you as your friend, but He shares His divine nature with you as your Savior and Lover of your soul.

The love of Christ surpasses knowledge. It surpasses any other experience you have in life. All experiences you have in your life will show your acceptance or nonacceptance of God's love for you. We are not to see Him as a Romeo but as our Lord and lover of our souls.

"As the Father has loved Me, so I have loved you," Jesus is telling you. God and Jesus were one from the beginning, together with the Holy Spirit. It was wonderful, the three of them ruling all and forming the earth, heavens, and all there is.

It is a union of love and power between Father and Son. God and God's Son and you—with God and in God's image. Can you see how precious you are? You are precious to God and precious within the law of love, which is life.

"Thy lovingkindness is better than life ..." the Psalmist wrote (Psalms 63:3). He knew and had meditated upon the person of God. Perhaps he had done what you are doing right now—repeating and meditating upon the beauty of the Lord, beholding His majesty, and basking in the might of His Word. His all-perfect love casts out fear. "... he who is afraid has not reached the full maturity of love— is not yet grown into love's complete perfection" (1 John 4:18 AMPLIFIED).

Not Building Fear Walls

Elizabeth was only six when her father left her mother. She decided that the same fate would never be hers. No man would ever do that to her. She made up her mind to be the most incredible, wonderful, adorable wife who ever lived. Any man would be insane to drop her. She married her high-school sweetheart in her third year of college, and after nine years of marriage, he moved out of the house and filed for divorce.

Elizabeth nearly lost her mind. That which she dreaded and feared had come upon her. The fear which had driven her for so many years had materialized.

When Elizabeth married her husband, she allowed her fears to control her thoughts. If he came home late from the office, she worried he was spending time with another woman. She rifled through his wallet and pockets at night, looking for clues about his behavior when he wasn't with her.

She worked obsessively, cleaning and keeping a spotless, attractive home. If he left his shoes in the middle of the floor, she took it as a sign of his indifference. ("Do you care that I spend all day cleaning this house?")

She began eating compulsively and gained weight. ("Can I help it? You're never home anymore.") When she was out with her husband, she clung to his arm and watched his face every time an attractive female passed by. Later she asked questions like, "Do you think I'm as pretty as the hatcheck girl?"

"What hatcheck girl?"

"You know very well. The one you kept looking at all night!"

Elizabeth's fears swelled and fed on each other. She built, day by day, a higher and thicker wall of fear around herself. Let's look at how she accomplished this.

Elizabeth's fears were:

1. Her husband might leave her, just as her father had left her mother. This, she told herself, would be absolutely dreadful; in fact, a fate worse than death.
2. Elizabeth was afraid that if she was rejected, she would be a total loser, because to be rejected was terrible. If she was rejected, that meant *she* was terrible.
3. She was afraid she wasn't capable of keeping her husband in love with her because maybe she wasn't worthy of being loved on a permanent basis.
4. If her husband were to stop loving her or be unfaithful to her, it would be a direct reflection of her self-worth. She told herself that if she lost her husband, her life would be worth nothing.

Elizabeth's fears tormented her. She would have to eliminate her self-defeating behaviors by resisting and standing against the irrational things she was telling herself. Those misbeliefs which she needed to realize and deal with were:

- To lose a person's love makes one a loser, therefore if I lose my husband's love, I'm a loser.

- It's terrible not to be able to control other people's feelings because they can be so fickle and untrustworthy.
- Suffering is bad, therefore if I suffer, I'm bad.

Elizabeth had not resisted these false pronunciations and therefore remained in the deadly trap of fear. Her expectations, then, enhanced by her misbeliefs and brought into reality by her thoughts, were:

- She *expected* her husband to eventually leave her.
- She *expected* to become the unlovable person she vowed she'd never be.
- She *expected* to fail at being a worthwhile person.

She overate and became worrisome and sickly. Fat and unhappy about herself, she nagged her husband, "You don't kiss me when you come home. Aren't I attractive to you?" She became jealous and vindictive, just waiting for the final blow, when he'd be unfaithful or drop her.

Elizabeth came to me for counseling when she was one hundred pounds overweight and riddled with a variety of physical ailments common to her emotional condition. I learned her husband was being treated for ulcers at the same time.

Through therapy Elizabeth saw what she was doing to herself and what she had done to her marriage. She had upset the children, as well as her husband, by teaching them how to feel guilty and manipulated.

Typical accusations of hers were, "You kids never do what I ask you to do! I live with little *slobs* around here!"

Elizabeth wasn't hopeless, though. Although unhappy, she was determined to change her life for the better. I asked her to make her own list of misbeliefs. Together we arrived at the following (Which of these self-destroying sentences sound familiar to you?):

1. Gaining and keeping somebody's love is the hardest thing on earth to do.
2. I have to be something really special in order to be loved. If I am not, the person who loves me is either an inferior-type person or he or she is somehow blinded to reality.
3. It's bad to have faults, therefore because I have faults, I'm bad.
4. I must work hard to earn a person's love, and the harder I work the more the other person owes it to me to love me.
5. I should be the only person in my spouse's life whom she or he is close to.
6. I should be the most vital interest in my spouse's life. Without me, his or her life ought to fall to pieces.
7. My spouse should share everything in life with me.
8. My spouse should be my best friend and only mine.

These and other misbeliefs were at the core of Elizabeth's unhappiness. She did eventually change for the better. In time, a soft, peaceful countenance replaced the harried and tormented one she had when she first walked into my office. She learned to replace the above with the truth by telling herself some new sentences every day. It was hard work. She had to begin first thing in the morning.

"First, I humble myself by telling myself I'm a Loved Person," she told me. "That's really hard to do. I've been too proud to accept God's love and consider myself important to Him. I wanted to *earn* importance. I believed only in my own interpretation of love, which was that you earned it."

She practiced replacing the false self-talk with the truth:

1. To be rejected is unpleasant, but it is not the worst thing that could happen. Everyone is rejected at some time or another. It comes with life. In Jesus Christ, I can handle it. I will never be rejected by Him because His love is the realm I choose to live within.

2. I do not have to labor at earning love. I'm lovable because God says so, and He's always right.
3. Nobody owes it to me to love me.
4. I do not have to be the "best." I give others the right to succeed over me.
5. I want my spouse to have other friends to enrich his or her life.
6. I do not insist that I be the most vital person in anyone's life.
7. I allow my husband or wife freedom to share with me what he or she chooses to share. I do not have to be in control of everything that happens.
8. Nobody on this earth belongs to me. Human beings are purposed from the beginning to love and serve God and Him only. I belong to the Lord and through Him I can love others sweetly and perfectly, with a heavenly love that allows and helps people to be who He called them to be. *To insist others belong to me alone is setting myself up as a false idol.*

Elizabeth's change, though marvelous, came too late to save her marriage. Her husband had already found himself a girl friend. One night, with a trailer hooked up to his car, he and his young girl friend took off for the wide-open spaces.

Elizabeth did not go to pieces. Instead, she joined a Bible-believing, Full Gospel church, read the Word of God, and prayed daily; she went to a weekly Bible study and never ceased praying for her husband.

A happy note to Elizabeth's story is that her husband did return to her after nearly a year of profligating. Theirs is a unique and heartwarming testimony. Her husband committed his life to Jesus as Elizabeth had, and they started a whole new life together. She forgave him with no contingencies attached. With counseling, good friends, Bible study, prayer, and the love of a dynamic fellowship of believers, they made it through a very difficult period of adjustment, forgiveness, and new growth. Fear was now gone. They trusted God.

Realize right now that fear is the enemy of faith.

Fear is your enemy.

Fear is an enemy of God. It's loveless.

God's love removes fear. Only His love is powerful enough to dispel it forever. Only His love casts it out. His perfect love gets rid of fear, and that kind of love is what you're living in. "Whoso keepeth his word, in him verily is the love of God perfected." So God is telling us that His perfect love is something *you* can have and know. You have it by keeping, doing, saying, having, being, sharing, and acting upon His Word.

> God's Word tells you that fear is to be cast out by love. Live in God's love realm of life, and you'll kick fear in the shins daily.

Fear always brings personal failure. No matter what you've achieved outwardly, if you're riddled with fear inside, you have essentially lost. What you win by defeating fear is tremendous.

Defeating Fear

A true story that thrills and challenges my heart is the following one about a great man of God from India named Sadhu Sundar Singh (told in *The Story of Sadhu Sundar Singh,* by Cyril Davey). It was around the year 1915, and the sadhu was between his many treks on foot to Tibet to preach the Gospel. He was staying with a friend in the Simla hills. After supper one evening they were sitting on the veranda when the sadhu slipped away across the lawn toward the garden to pray. He stood alone in deep prayer, gazing across the valley to the villages in the distance.

Suddenly the man on the veranda lunged to his feet in terror. He was helpless to aid the sadhu. It was too late to get a gun. He didn't dare shout. Unknown to the praying man, a wild leopard was creeping toward him from behind the trees at the side of the garden. Its tail was outstretched, its belly almost touching the ground in typical attack posture. As it was about to pounce, the sadhu turned quietly and, seeing the animal, stretched out his hand and motioned it to come forward. The leopard rose, moved forward, and sat beside the sadhu while he continued to pray. He prayed on and on, stroking the head of the wild beast at his side. The leopard swayed slightly, and now and again looked up at the praying man.

When Sundar turned to return to the house, the leopard's powerful form was lost to sight among the trees again. This wasn't even an unusual experience for Sadhu Sundar Singh. It was, to this great Christian man, an everyday happening in his life. Would you consider Sadhu Sundar Singh a man who lived in fear or in the power of the Holy Spirit?

"As the Father loves Jesus, so does He love you." *Right this minute.* Joshua 1:8 says, "This book of the law shall not depart out of thy mouth; but thou shalt meditate therein day and night. . . ." That means the Word which you are digesting into your heart and soul and speaking to yourself. You won't allow Jesus' Word to leave you. Don't you let it leave. It is truth. Perfect love casts out fear.

Keep the Word. Meditate on it day and night. The Word of the Lord is forever. Jesus loves you as much as the Father loves Him. Face it: you're a Loved Person. You have absolutely nothing to fear.

the choice

i do not fear
because You rose from the dead,
        because that fierce one, that one
                called death,
        could not hold You.
because You are
        as alive now as in
        those days in Galilee,
because You chose to spend Yourself
        on us, dispensing Your Spirit,
                Holy and great,
        to lead us in all things

,i do not fear.

        stretched before me
                are shining plains of love
                ,golden fruits
                        waiting.

        i move hungrily forward
                        and,
                because death could not hold
        You

        i live
        i live on the plains
          the shining plains

                wearing my crown,
                dressed in faith as simple
                        yet triumphant as the dawn,
        because i
                have chosen You,
fear
        runs from me
        because
                it looks at me
                and sees
                        You

10

Facing Loneliness

I have asked many people, including ministers and well-known Christian leaders, how they have coped with loneliness in their lives, and to what degree they have experienced loneliness.

One of the most frank and sobering conversations I have had was with a nationally known Christian speaker, a woman whose ministry had touched thousands of lives across the world.

"Marie," she told me, "I've been so lonely that I could do nothing but cry for days on end. I've cried so hard my eyes would be practically shut and my skin would continually be red and blotched."

I looked at her sitting beside me on the speakers' platform, a picture of success and confidence. Her happy face showed no signs of ever having been blotched and tear-stained.

"You? Lonely?" I asked. She sighed and smiled. "One day I was feeling so lonely I went driving in my car, opened the window, and screamed as loud as I could until my voice gave out and I collapsed at the wheel, hoarse and choking like a person half-drowned."

I listened, amazed, as she continued. "I was a Christian, I taught Sunday school, I loved the Lord, but I was desolate and miserable. I prayed the Lord would forgive me, but

I just couldn't seem to escape the constant horror of loneliness."

She told me how she experienced days when she would get up in the morning and go right back to bed again. She stayed there all day hiding and crying. Outside her window the sun would be shining on a beautiful spring day, but she would be rolled up in a clump under a blanket with the windows shut, sobbing and sighing like an infant screaming for a feeding.

You may ask how it is possible for a Christian to be so lonely. Isn't that a paradox? Didn't the Lord Himself tell us, "I will never leave you nor forsake you"? How can we be lonely if *He* is with us? Have you ever wondered if it is contradictory to love the Lord but at the same time suffer deep emotional pain and be lonely?

An usher in a large church once told me, "Since I retired I get so lonely at times, the silence around me is like a furnace."

A minister in the Midwest told me, "When my wife isn't with me, I get so lonely, especially at night, I feel as if nothing is important anymore. Everything becomes colorless and drab."

"I'm lonely now that the kids have gone to college."

"I'm lonely in a strange town."

"Since my husband left me," a woman of forty-three told me, "I have actually felt as if I were going to die of loneliness. I have felt anger and hurt, yes, but the worst pain is loneliness."

Have you ever felt so alone that even your toes hurt? "Lord, I'm so alone!" we may cry.

But are we really alone?

You pray and ask, "Lord, if You say You'll never leave me or forsake me, what am I doing wrong? Why do I become a blubbering mess at the absence of people or a person? What's wrong?"

The Lord in His faithfulness answers, "I have loved thee with an everlasting love: therefore with lovingkindness have I drawn thee" (Jeremiah 31:3).

"But Lord, how can You call this love? Look at the misery—"

He speaks again: "The Lord is near to the brokenhearted, And saves those who are crushed in spirit" (Psalms 34:18 NAS).

"But Lord, how is a person supposed to overcome loneliness? What do You expect of us?"

His voice is gentle, kind. "The righteous cry, and the Lord heareth, and delivereth them out of all their troubles" (Psalms 34:17).

To Be Delivered, Decide and Do!

There is a way out. When you're feeling like a dishrag in the dishpan of life, remember that if you're a child of God, you don't have to stay there.

The Lord is there beside you. "For I the Lord thy God will hold thy right hand, saying unto thee, Fear not; I will help thee" (Isaiah 41:13).

Delivering us out of troubles is a work God does for us. We help Him accomplish this for us by making some decisions.

The first step to deliverance is *decide*. You don't have to be a victim of loneliness anymore. The conference speaker who suffered loneliness so intensely decided one day that she didn't have to stay lonely. The action she took was vital: she *decided* to stop thinking and acting lonely.

You can't accomplish very much in life without making decisions. Even doing nothing takes a decision.

Realize there is a difference between boredom and loneliness. If you're bored you can create something exciting for yourself. You can also do the same if you're lonely, but you must first decide.

Decide now. Say out loud, "I will not fear, the Lord is with me. The Lord is my God. He strengthens me. Yes, He helps me. He upholds me with the right hand of His righteousness. I am a Loved Person! I am important to God and never, ever alone!"

Now go a step further and say out loud, "I refuse loneliness in the mighty name of Jesus. I refuse to live within its ugly claws. I will not be a victim of loneliness. I will be a complete person in myself. I will lift myself up in the name of Jesus and I *will* be happy again, I *will* be joyful, I *will* know power and peace in my life, because the Lord is the strength of my life!"

There was a time in my life when I told myself I was a castaway, a reject, a total zero, a blotch on the face of life. Finally, I had to force myself to hear what God had to say about the situation. I had been crying and pleading with Him and not waiting for His voice. I had been interpreting the events of life on my own, and my desperate prayers were getting me nowhere. I had to *decide* to listen to Him!

"You say You're a God of love, Lord," I cried out one day. "I don't feel one bit loved. Please show me where I'm wrong because I know You're right, just, and perfect. You are all truth and goodness."

I asked His forgiveness for grieving longer than I should have and for putting myself down so horribly. Again and again His Word to me was, "I have loved thee with an everlasting love: therefore with lovingkindness have I drawn thee."

I had to stand up on my two trembling legs before God,

all alone, without defense, and say, "Lord, I am going to accept this love of Yours."

I said, "I am now deciding to stop being lonely. As of this moment, I will not agonize anymore! I make this decision in the name of Jesus Christ, who is my refuge and my fortress! Lift up my hands which hang down, Lord, and strengthen my weak knees. I now decide to be all I can be in Your name, and I'll not wallow around as a lonely, unhappy person for one more minute! Amen!"

I said these words loud and clear so I could hear them in my own ears. I marched up and down in my living room, reading the Word of God out loud to myself.

It sank in. And it will sink in for you, too. Let God talk to you. *Decide* to be free. Your first step to being free of loneliness is making that decision.

Second, *do* something about your decision.

Most people feel lonely once in a while. Your husband or wife may be out of town, your children go away to camp, or a friend is gone on vacation, and you experience loneliness. Loneliness is not always a drastic emotional upheaval. Sometimes you may feel lonely just hearing a song that reminds you of a bygone happy time. Realize it's okay to feel lonely at times. Don't lie to yourself about it. It's not a social disgrace to be lonely. The absence of something you want causes you to feel lonely. You can handle it because you have the greatest power on earth and in heaven living *in* you.

Feeling blue because someone you love is not around is natural. Tell yourself it's okay to feel that way and give yourself the right to feel blue once in a while. But if you are trapped in a vise of anguish, get out, and get out *now*. Decide and *do*.

Popular psychology will tell you if you're lonely, join a

club, make a friend, go out on a date, take up hobbies, go back to school, and on and on. These may help alleviate boredom but may not effect a lasting cure for loneliness. It's not learning how to engage in outward activities that I'm talking about in this book. I'm talking about the action you take within your heart. Change your heart and you change your whole world.

Decide to walk in your deliverance and then *do* it.

Your personhood is settled in Jesus Christ. Therefore you don't make demands upon life and people to bring you the happiness and contentment you desire.

Doing is setting people free from being the source of your happiness.

Doing is releasing yourself from needing certain circumstances before you can be happy.

Doing is taking the Word of God and making your decision to believe it is wholly and unequivocably alive and real.

Doing is changing your self-talk if it is not true.

Instead Of	*You Speak the Truth*
I just can't go on without ————————.	I feel lonely without ————————, but I can carry on as a whole and fulfilled person in spite of the loss.

A man of about sixty years I'll call Monty came to me after seeing me on television and said, "You talk about being a Loved Person and about finding your completion in Christ, but I just can't seem to get it together. I try, but since my wife died, I'm so lonely and depressed, I just can't shake it. It's been five years now."

Grief and hurt are emotions we all experience when we lose a loved one, and as painful as it is, we can't avoid or run away from them. Five years is too long to grieve, though. There comes a time when we put our tears in a box with the scrapbooks and the memories and we say, "I will cherish you forever but now I will get on with the business of life."

When my dad was killed in a train accident in 1971, I lost a love that could never be replaced. I grieved over his loss and couldn't imagine life without a dad. Now, years later, my father's picture still stands near my typewriter, his letters are still in a drawer, and I respect his memory deeply. The grief and anguish of his loss are gone, however. I put the grief of his loss aside. I got on with the business of living.

The important message here is, I *decided* to be a fulfilled, happy person in spite of personal loss. I decided to be happy and fulfilled in Jesus Christ and that through Him, I could *do* it! He did the rest.

Loneliness and Your Self-Talk

I had to learn to change my self-talk.

Monty, the man lamenting the loss of his wife, needed to change his self-talk, too. He needed to look at the Word of God and see what God had to say about his situation and life. Did his words and God's words sound anything alike?

Hurting Words	*The Word of God*
There's no hope for me. I can't start over. I'm so lost and lonely.	He who has begun a good work in me will perform it until the day of Jesus Christ! (Philippians 1:6.) I can do all things through Christ who strengthens me! (Philippians 4:13.) I am complete in Christ! (Colossians 2:10.)

Monty spent several sessions with me and then months passed with no news from him. Not long ago I received a letter from Monty. No letter has ever thrilled me more. "I am a Loved Person!" he wrote ecstatically. "I know I am loved now. I tell myself every day how important I am to God. I feel comfortable speaking this way because I know it's what God is saying to me through His Word. I can't thank God enough for what He has done for me. Every day I feel more secure in Him. Thanks, Marie."

Why Am I Lonely?

One reason we may suffer so intensely when alone is the popular notion that alone means lonely. We're *taught* to be lonely. We confuse boredom with loneliness.

Ever notice how you think you're *supposed* to be lonely if certain circumstances or relationships are not present in your life? We feel obliged to be lonely if, for example, somebody isn't in love with us or if the telephone doesn't ring for a week or if everybody we know is going somewhere Friday night and we're sitting home with nothing but a bowl of popcorn for company.

Who says you have to be lonely just because there's nobody around to talk to? Where do you read in the Bible, "Thou shalt be lonely if there's nobody around to talk to"?

Jesus says, "Pray without ceasing," and in the Old Testament we read the words of God, "Come, let us reason together." Jesus says He will never leave or forsake us. Do you speak *His* Words or your own negative, misery-laden words every time you open your mouth?

If you're sitting like a lump in loneliness soup, I want you to examine your self-talk. What are you telling yourself? Are you telling yourself any of the following?

Nobody loves me.
Nobody ever will love me.
Everybody else has more fun than I have.
Other people have more friends than I do and that's terrible.
Other people aren't as lonely as I am.

All of the above are lies. Can you identify the lies you are telling yourself?

It is nonsense to believe nobody loves you. You're a lovable, marvelous person and if you took the time to think about it, you'd know it. The truth is, the people in your life at the moment may not be giving you the love you think you need and want. A man once told me, "Marie, everybody at church tells me they love me. 'Oh, I just love you, brother,' they say, but they have never invited me to dinner. I'd rather they didn't love me so much so they'd have me over for dinner!"

Are you telling yourself, "Nobody loves me" (a lie) when actually God loves you to pieces? Replace the lie with the truth: "I make myself unhappy when God doesn't do what I tell Him and people don't love me the way I want them to."

You're such a precious person—you really are. The Lord is standing there by your side now, loving you and helping you right where your need is. He wants you to be free of every negative and destructive thought that could bring you agony and hurt. He is your Deliverer. He delivers you from yourself and your own hurtful thinking patterns.

Teaching yourself not to be lonely means you teach yourself to replace the lying self-talk in which you have engaged in the past with the *truth*.

- Even though I feel unloved, I know that I am lovable and that God is loving me unconditionally right now.
- I give myself the right to have fun in the Lord not based on how much fun others are having.
- It is not terrible that other people have more friends than I have. My happiness does not depend upon how many friends other people have.
- I am not a ship of woe isolated on the great iceberg of life. Others may be in that boat, but praise God, I'm bailing out because there's dry land ahead!
- People always love me because the love of the Lord is within me, drawing people to me.

Teach yourself to be fulfilled in Jesus instead of feeling lonely. No relationship can compare with it, and all your other relationships will be a result of it.

B.C.

I knew loneliness
before.
Barren, scalding
loneliness.
When scorpions devoured the days
and the nights,
when time
screamed by
in heaps of rubbish
on the way to the
dump.
When my life
lay gnarled and severed
in a bag of
rags.
I knew loneliness
before.
I knew loneliness when
I ached
so passionately
to mean a little something
to
     someone.

But now
let me tell you,
the crushing weight
of loneliness
will never touch my life
        again
because the Master Jesus
has claimed me for His
own.

I am His
    someone.

11

Beyond Lonely

If you insist that having the love of friends and relatives is of dire necessity to your personal happiness, then you are bound to find yourself alone without your demands met. You're a sitting duck for misery and loneliness.

It's true that friends and loved ones are wonderful gifts of God, but more important to your personal happiness is that *you* love. If you believe every person should have a loving family around them at all times, then you may suffer loneliness should they be too busy to include you in their lives.

If you tell yourself you can't live without something or someone, you'll suffer untold loneliness without it or that person. Remember, it's okay to be lonely at times. It's okay to miss someone who or something that has been special to you. It's okay as long as you are in control of your feelings.

Allow yourself a certain length of time to feel bad. An example is, "Okay, I feel bad about Marge and Fred moving to Walla Walla. I will devote Tuesday to thinking about them and feeling very sorry for myself. I'll try not to think about anything else that day. On Wednesday I will go about my business and although I miss them, I will not become immobilized with loneliness at this loss."

Lie	*Truth*
My old friends have moved and new ones are so hard to make.	I can be a friend to others. I can befriend the people at my church. I can choose to be a blessing to others and feel good about my friendships.

Take charge of your emotions. Decide and *do*. Decide that it is not terrible to feel lonely at times, but that you will not be a victim of anguish and desperation caused by unbridled feelings of isolation and loss. You're in charge. Face your feelings in the light of God's Word.

You *can* live without cherished people and things. You *can* live a fulfilled and exciting life, even without the things you thought were of dire necessity to your personal happiness. You are in charge of your emotions and feelings. Circumstances do not control your emotions. Situations do not, and neither do your relationships and the events of life.

The Apostle John, a Man With Problems

A biblical character who certainly fits our Loved Person description is John. He was once known as the "son of thunder," full of fire and storm, but he became the apostle of love and peace. He referred to himself as the disciple Jesus loved best, and his writings are the most intimate of all inspired writings, next to the Song of Solomon. At the end of his life he was alone, condemned to a desolate island in exile.

John was a man of intense hatred before he became a disciple of Jesus. Even after traveling with Jesus and living side by side with Him, John's old nature constantly needed tempering by the love of God.

Some people might wonder how a man like John, who

had once been intolerant, vengeful, and vindictive, could also have been "the disciple whom Jesus loved," as John wrote of himself.

Jesus' love surpasses the love of man, and John came to understand that. He was a bona fide Loved Person. He knew he was loved in spite of himself. He knew Jesus saw beyond his faults, and he readily received the holy love Jesus offered.

John's life was long and filled with trials as well as glories. He saw his beloved Lord crucified on the cross, was persecuted by Saul of Tarsus, and later became a co-worker with him. Under wicked Herod Agrippa, John saw his brother James martyred with the sword. John was persecuted under Domitian, and tradition tells how he was taken to Rome and put into boiling oil. He was then sent to labor in the mines and finally to exile on the island of Patmos. It was this man who recorded Jesus' words, "Let not your heart be troubled, neither let it be afraid" (John 14:27).

This is the man who wrote, "He that overcometh shall inherit all things . . ." (Revelation 21:7). This is the man who, as the spiritual father of the believers of Ephesus, wrote to them as little children, saying, "Behold, what manner of love the Father hath bestowed upon us, that we should be called the sons of God . . ." (1 John 3:1).

Love is more than feelings, more than knowledge, more than experience. On Patmos, the Apostle John, this "pillar in the church," this eagle and closest friend of the Lord Jesus Christ, wore loneliness as he had worn his sufferings, like a crown. "It is in silence and solitude that spirits attain their complete beauty," writes F. B. Meyer. John learned there is a depth of loneliness that penetrates the cloudy substance of sorrow. In perfect union with Jesus Christ, it is transformed to the sublime.

The boiling oil left John unharmed. The labors in the mines at Patmos left him wearied and physically broken, and his years of exile were endured as an old man. In looking at the life of this great man of God, you can see the many lonely hours he must have known.

John's circumstances often looked quite bleak. There were times when the future seemed hopeless. There were also times when the present was unbearable. But John was filled with the power of loving. The Holy Spirit made John a love-man, and love *never* fails.

This apostle of love was to know Jesus as no other human being ever would. In recording the Apocalypse, he unfolded to humanity that which was previously hidden or unknown and that which is to come. How appropriate that this man of love be given this final revelation to humankind.

The same God who transformed and revolutionized John's life with His love is at work now in your life and mine.

> *You* are in control of you.

Using the Skills of Coping

So you're lonely. You're sad. How are you going to cope? Can you say openly and freely, "Lord Jesus, I give You all that I am and all that I feel"?

- I am feeling lonely so I give loneliness to You to do something beautiful with it.
- I am feeling sad so I give it to You to transform into something good instead of negative and destructive.

I believe that in our hour of deepest sorrow, God can speak to us most lucidly. When you're coping with loneliness, you first of all should look at your interpretation of loneliness. There are varied ideas of what the particular feeling is. One person may think it's when all his or her friends are gone for the weekend, while others live desolate lives, isolated and forgotten for years. Their loneliness is like an old coat they wear night and day.

Give God the glory of your aloneness, whatever its depth. Make your loneliness *your* island of Patmos. Let God speak to you. Let Him touch you with Himself—let Him love you.

In His Presence Is Fullness of Joy

You will experience fullness of joy in your most intimate moments with God. When He wishes to speak some private, personal truth to you, it will usually be when you are alone with Him and listening; it will be when He has your full attention.

Fullness of joy is better than contentment. In it, all the peace offered to man is embraced.

Wait happily before God in those hours alone with Him. Let yourself be submitted totally to Him and His comforting presence. In a position of complete resignation to God, the devil flees. The devil is removed and cannot tease or deceive you. He cannot pervert your interpretation of suffering. You're in charge now. You're spending your love on God.

God will separate you for a time so that He can minister to you, teach you, develop you through His Word and by His Spirit. These are the times you may kick your heels angrily and wonder where the party went. You need those seasons of isolation with God in order to get more fully educated in His language. If you had a choice of best friends, one who lived down the block and spoke your language or a fellow who lived in a foreign country and spoke a language you never heard of, which one would you choose?

You choose how you will spend your emotions. If you decide to spend them in the pursuit of your own selfish desires for happiness, you will only hurt yourself. Selfish people find it unbearable to be alone with God for any extended period of time. They are the persons C. S. Lewis wrote about as "... those pathetic people who simply want friends and can never make any. The very condition of having friends is that we should want something else besides friends."

The Loved Person wants a relationship with God above all else. Once we have this, we have everything. Our hearts are so entwined with His, so in tune with His heartbeat, that our emotions become His to control. This is the perfect place for them.

You are a person of many wonderful emotions. Allow God to express Himself through you. Enjoy your feelings because they're blessed by the Lord. He is positive and loving, and so are you.

thank you, Lord

for feelings
,for my own special
unique
feelings
. they're important
to me
and so i know they're
important
to You
,too.
i give them to You
because i want You
to enjoy
me
and enjoy my
feelings
as we celebrate
the life of Christ in me
together
with nothing
ugly or negative
separating
my emotions
from
        Yours

12

Love Does Not Seek to Control

Love always includes risk. When you love somebody, you become vulnerable. The love and respect you have for yourself is neither vain nor pride filled, and that gives you power to drop defensive behaviors. You recognize God's perfect design and purpose for you, seeing your intrinsic value to Him and the cherished position you hold in His heart.

The fear of being hurt often causes a person to want to control his or her relationships with others. Intense difficulties arise because most people don't like being controlled. If they do, they need as much help as the one doing the controlling.

Because you can accept yourself, you are able to accept another. This does not mean that you love with blind eyes and refuse to see any faults or problems. Approaching these problems, you are not vexed with pride, self-pity, desire to control, or anger, because as a Loved Person you allow your world to be big enough to include the right to be hurt occasionally.

Wanting to Control

Carl was a well-respected engineer who worked for a large company. He was engaged to Mavis, an attractive secretary he had known since high school. They seemed like a compatible couple, but as the wedding date neared, Carl worried that maybe he was making a mistake. I asked him what problems he felt were insurmountable.

"It's just that we argue so much. I'm worried about it because it seems as though every time we're together we fight."

He insisted he loved Mavis, but he had serious doubts about whether their marriage would stand a chance. After talking awhile, we made a discovery together. It was something Carl had never faced before. He approached marriage and romance in much the same way as he worked with machinery on the job. That is, he expected to control things as though he were operating a machine.

Carl expected Mavis to do things the way he wanted, to be the way he wanted her to be, and to make no problems for him. He expected her to be there when he wanted her to be, and if she didn't always perform smoothly and predictably, he was upset. Arguments would follow, and he never dreamed he was any part of the cause of the conflict.

Relationships are often conflicts of power: Who is going to control whom? Some drastic misconceptions of love are: "If you're my friend, you'll let me rule you without putting up an argument."

"If you love me, you'll never hurt or disappoint me."

"If you really love me, you'll let me dominate you."

When these demands aren't met, the unhappy conclusion is, "I'm unlucky in love." Or, "I just can't seem to find the

right girl [guy]." Or, "All men are rats." ("All women are
opportunists.")

We set ourselves up to hurt and be hurt.

Married partners may believe, "Since you're married to
me, you owe it to me to make my needs more important to
you than your own."

A son or daughter insists, "You're my parent. You're supposed to sacrifice all for me."

These demands, often unspoken, placed upon others, can
result in frustration and conflict, and will preclude such
words as, "You don't care about me. You don't love me."

Or, even worse: "You are not enough. *I need more.*"

You're hitting your head against the wall of futility.

You need Jesus Christ and the liberating power of *His*
love. When His love really and truly rules your emotions
and thoughts, you can give people the right to live and love,
even if it is not the to-the-death dedication you crave.

Carl and Mavis entered into therapy together and man-
aged to work through their problems based on some very
sound scriptural principles. Their first assignment was to
read 1 John 4:7–11 at least once a day. Mavis recognized
that she responded to Carl's controlling spirit with anger
much the same as she felt toward her mother, who had also
tried to control her life. Not knowing how to cope with their
feelings, they nearly lost each other. Their story has a happy
ending, but many stories do not end so well.

There's another type of controlling and it's motivated by a
forceful craving for love. When love is craved so hungrily,
pursued and ached for, it is usually not found. Jesus said we
are to lose our lives if we are to gain our lives. That means,
we put someone else's highest good above our own (agape
love). We aren't seeking to fulfill our own lusts, hungers,

and cravings—we are dedicated to being a blessing to others.

There is a person who *craves* love. He is desperate for it, has to have it, lives for it, and goes nuts without it. He's:

The Love Addict

The dictionary defines *crave* as: "To have an intense desire for; to need urgently, require; to beg earnestly for; implore."

When you *crave* something, you're like an addict. You live for the thing craved; you're desperate for it. Your very life depends on it. Without it you're unhappy.

When you crave a person's devotion to affirm your own sense of value in life, when your existence is just nothing without someone else's pledge of love for you, you're hooked, addicted. God didn't create you to be an addict, to be dependent upon others for all your love and self-worth. He created you to be free to feel the full gamut of human emotion and to give the full expression of your personality to the world and those around you while enjoying yourself. He created you to develop your life in Him. No other person is to define your personhood but God.

Allow people to enhance your life, but not control it. Often a controller is not even aware of what he or she is doing. We may try to control others for our own gain and when the desired results aren't accomplished, we get furious about it.

Take Mimi, a thirty-three-year-old church secretary. She fell desperately in love (she said) with an assistant pastor in her church. Oh, how she adored him. She followed him around everywhere he went. She was at every meeting he ministered at. She volunteered to type all his notes, papers, and letters, even though his department had a secretary. She worked passionately, trying to make herself needed in his life. After several months of clinging to him and working herself to a frazzle to get him to care for her, he announced his engagement to another girl.

"The rat! The chauvinist! The bum!" Mimi raged over lunch one day. She began to cry, dripping bitter tears on her cheeseburger.

"Why do you say he's all those things?" I asked.

"Don't you see how he *used* me?" she sniffed. "I thought he cared about me!"

Mimi had some misconceptions about love and I hoped she would, in time, see them. Some of them were:

- When I love somebody he ought to love me back!
- What I want I ought to get!
- When I work extra hard to get somebody to care about me, he had better care about me, or else!
- To get somebody of the opposite sex to love me, I have to really work hard at it.
- People who get what *I* want (and don't get) are usually phonies; they get those things denied me by devious, sneaky means.

Mimi truly believed that the assistant pastor owed it to her to care about her since, after all, she was working full-time and overtime to earn this love.

She approached the relationship the way someone might go about getting a job promotion: "If I work hard and show I'm really serious, the boss will give me the promotion." Or, "If I create a need for my services, I'll get a raise." Mimi was more involved with Mimi's abilities than a giving and caring relationship with a man. Mimi wanted to have love on her terms, to be gotten her way, and if it didn't turn out the way she figured it should, it was all *his* fault, the rat.

Manipulative behavior is always hurtful. The manipulator tries to get his or her own way by inducing guilt in another or by creating an untoward need or dependency either for someone else or upon himself. Mimi manipulated for her own way and lost. The man she wanted was a human being with thoughts, dreams, and feelings of his own, not a machine doing only as it's told.

Your relationships with people are not mechanical. People change, make mistakes, and do hurtful things at times. They don't always do exactly what you want them to. They may reject you at times, move away, not write, forget your birthday. They have the right to live and be in God's world with God as their God, and not you.

- Are you desperately clinging to, craving, or desiring some person to affirm your personhood?
- Is it a *person* who holds the strings of your self-worth?
- Are you trying to control a relationship by manipulation or by working too hard to earn love?

Love or approval of people does not add one iota to your inherent worth. Many people suffering from depression are people who are loved by other people. Yet they remain depressed and miserable.

If you really accept the fact that your self-worth depends upon God's opinion of you, you will put your efforts in the right place. Instead of making mistakes, hurting yourself, and becoming bitter, you will live free and content because before your heart goes out to another, it's already been consumed by and hidden in Christ. Then all you do and care for are *through* Jesus, not outside Him.

Here is another example of unsuccessful manipulation.

I'll call the wife Marsha. Marsha is upset because John, her husband, is going on another business trip. It's the third one in two months. She tells her girl friend (whose husband never goes on business trips) how she wishes she had a husband like hers. "I wonder if John really loves me. During the first seven years of our married life, he never went out of town once. Now all of a sudden he's buying attaché cases and matching luggage. I have a feeling it's the beginning of the end."

Obsessed relationships are not of the Lord. Food addicts, drug addicts, alcohol addicts are no worse off than the love addict. Nowhere in the Bible does it say, "If thou shalt take a wife unto thy bosom, thou shalt never go on a business trip and furthermore, thou shalt do all that she demands of you, no matter how neurotic those demands are, because you ought to be cleaving in the manner she says."

Here is a sampling of Marsha and John's conversation at home:

MARSHA (*sweetly*) John, must you go on this trip?

JOHN   Honey, you know I have to. It's important to the company and it's important to me.

MARSHA (*softly*) Lucky's husband never goes on trips.

JOHN   I know he doesn't, honey. His job is different from mine.

MARSHA (*sighing*) Ah, they are so in love. They're like honeymooners. And to think they've been married longer than we have.

JOHN   Marsha, will you help me pack my shirts?

MARSHA (*coyly*) Little Johnny was hoping you'd play handball with him tomorrow.

JOHN   I'll play handball with him on Saturday.

MARSHA   (*sadly*) Of course, little Suzie will cry for her daddy.

JOHN   Never mind the shirts. I'll pack them myself.

MARSHA   (*stoically*) And I'll be alone with the kids, with that back door still not fixed. And the tires on the car are low on air.

JOHN   Where's my shaving lotion?

MARSHA   (*trembling*) Heaven help me if I get another one of those obscene phone calls. Do you think someone could be stalking our house? (John opens and slams cabinet doors in the bathroom in search of his shaving lotion.)

MARSHA   (*suddenly*) John, have we made out a will? Suppose something were to happen to me? What would happen to the children? Have you thought about that, John?

JOHN   Marsha, was little Johnny playing with my shaving lotion or what? I can't find it.

MARSHA   (*martyrishly*) I feel an asthma attack coming on. Oh, dear, my left arm is getting numb. I've got cramps in my chest. My Lord, there's a lump in my breast.

JOHN   Does this mean you can't drive me to the airport?

MARSHA   (*explosively*) You haven't heard a word I've said. You don't love me, do you? You don't care if I die tonight, do you? Well, I've got news for you, Mr. Matching Luggage, I feel an asthma attack coming on and if I die, just give me a plain and simple funeral and have the preacher say, "Here was a woman who lived and died for her man, who insisted on his business trip!"

We cannot manipulate people for our own way. We can't manipulate God, either.

The Bible teaches us that through the law of love we enter into the promise of God and the happiness we long for. If we handle our love lives with our families, friends, and spouses as manipulators and love addicts, how can we expect to really pierce the heart of God with our godliness?

Let's look at some of the misbeliefs we harbor when we want others to do as we wish:

- My needs are the most important things in the whole world.
- If you enter my world you must live by my rules.
- It's your responsibility to make me happy and fulfilled.
- If you fail me, you are at fault.

Marsha, the distraught wife, used several ploys you may have recognized. She tried wooing her huband out of the idea of going out of town, making him fccl guilty about it, getting his pity, and lastly, resorted to getting sick. If all else failed, she could always die. That would really show him.

Let's take a closer look at the use of physical illness as a way of manipulating others.

Getting Your Way by Being Ill

Sickness has traditionally been an acceptable way to get attention. It has been approved of by church and state, and so we've allowed it to sneak into our life-style as though it belonged there.

Sickness is not an acceptable means to get your own way. You ought to fight against sickness the way you'd fight insects taking over your home. Fight against sickness in the power of the Holy Spirit, with the sword of the Word. For too long sickness and disease have been invited into our

Christian homes and families in the guise of "suffering for God." Ridiculous!

Jesus died on the cross to pay the penalty for sickness as well as sin. First Peter 2:24 says, "Who his own self bare our sins in his own body on the tree, that we, being dead to sins, should live unto righteousness: by whose stripes ye were healed."

Psalm 103 tells us that one of the benefits God provides is to heal all of our diseases. If you will take to heart what I am telling you and do the things I am outlining here, you *will* find yourself walking in physical health.

- Set yourself free from manipulating others with sickness.
- Set yourself free from avoiding situations or people by getting sick.
- Set yourself free from fear because fear can resort to sickness in order to justify itself.

Soak yourself in the Word of God. *"Whoso keepeth his word,* in him verily is the love of God perfected" (1 John 2:5, my italics).

Keeping His Word means to meditate on it, say it, and do it. In order to do it, you have to know it. In order to know it, you have to say it. Speak the words of the Lord out loud to yourself: "Lord, in the name of Jesus I refuse to manipulate others by becoming sick."

Colossians 2:10 reads, "And ye are complete in him, which is the head of all principality and power."

Say out loud, "I am complete in Jesus Christ, who is the head of all principality and power."

Don't stop saying these life-giving words of truth to yourself. Say them again and again until you've saturated your soul with them. "I am complete in Christ Jesus. I have been made full and have come to the fullness of life!"

Understand that your needs are not the most important things in the world. Your needs (and wants) are important, but not more important than anyone else's.

If Marsha gets sick enough, John might cancel his business trip; at least, that's what Marsha is hoping. Maybe she is not consciously planning to get sick. Maybe she did not sit down and tell herself, *At half-past two this afternoon I'm going to have an aneurysm while folding John's shirts,* but her actions showed what is in her mind. It's the "you'll do what I want or else" ploy of the enemy. It is not God's way.

Love Without a Price Tag

The Lord is showing us how to love unconditionally. The Lord is showing us that we are so precious to Him, we can afford to throw our lives into His care and trust Him to love us. The Lord is teaching us gently and carefully by His spirit how to live whole and healthy lives, giving the best to those around us through knowing that we ourselves are God's best. We're Christians!

You are a Loved Person and you can help your mate pack, bid him or her bon voyage, and pray that he or she has a blessed and successful trip. You will miss your mate, but you're not awash with gloom at his or her absence. Loved Persons don't cloy and manipulate for love. You're free to love for real.

Loved Persons dare to say, regarding relationships, "You can live without me and I can live without you, even though I love you and you love me. We're in God's orchestra together. We make beautiful harmony which only the two of us can make and it's heavenly, but sometimes we play solos. I can appreciate your solo."

You're living in the law of God's love as His Loved Person. When you say, "I love you," there's no price tag attached. You don't punish or charge for your love with guilt-invoking accusations: "If you had gotten to the restaurant on time, we could have gotten a decent table."

"It drives me crazy when you don't put the cap back on the toothpaste."

"I wait all week for the weekend so I can be with you, and you spend it in front of the TV set watching the ball game."

"After all this time you don't know I like pizza without anchovies?"

"You make me angry."

"You always hurt my feelings."

"You don't love me."

"You don't care."

When love is obsessive, the wrath incurred when demands go unmet is fierce, deadly. Remember Mimi's biting words: "He's a chauvinist, a rat, a bum." Why such labels? Because the object of her obsession didn't do what she wanted him to do, didn't produce what she demanded. *He didn't love her.* So he's a bum.

There is a misplacement of affection here. Knowing how to love others requires knowing how to determine where others fit in our lives. There is a simple method of placing relationships in their proper perspective, and the next chapter will show us how.

special somebodys

We all have somebody to love
            ,Lord
,when we are Yours,
            even if we are prisoners
in a place where we see
            nobody
because
this family of ours is
            as wide
                        as the swept-new skies
and we are more than
            forever can count.
Children of the Lord God
                        shall fill the heavens
rejoicing
                        and thanking our King
                                    for so many
                        somebodys
                                    to love,
even, Lord,
            the somebodys
who are not numbered in God's family
            of stars
,whose music is not
            familiar to the angels
these are
            special somebodys
                        —the special somebodys
            God has us
                        to love.

13

You and Your Relationships

Manny is a middle-aged computer programmer. He is terribly upset. He has made himself quite nervous and frustrated. "Nobody listens when I talk," he complains. "People just ignore me lately when I start a conversation. I'm really a loser."

"Which people are you talking about?" I ask.

"What do you mean, *which* people?" he mumbles angrily. "All people."

"Who are *all* people?"

"Oh, all right, since you're going to be so picky, this morning on the bus I started talking to the man sitting next to me and he all but changed seats. Then when I got to work I struck up a conversation on the elevator and not a soul responded. At lunch I told the receptionist a joke I thought was hilarious and she barely smiled. People just turn away when they see me coming, I'm telling you!"

"How about your wife? Does she turn away when you talk to her?"

"Well, no. That is, not all the time—"

"How about that buddy of yours, the one you bowl with? Does he turn away when you tell him a favorite joke?"

"No—"

"And how about the people in your office—the ones you

work side by side with every day? Do they turn away when you start a conversation?"

"Oh, they're pretty friendly. I mean, we get along."

"So what you're telling me is that you're upset with people you don't know because they don't treat you like a close friend."

Manny just needs to identify the areas of relationships in his life. Let's look at these areas. Think of a circle divided into four distinct rings. The outer ring, **D,** is a fairly large one. The rings then get smaller until the very inner ring, **A,** which is the smallest.

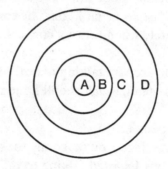

Let's look at each ring individually.

1. *The D Ring:* This is the outside ring, the biggest one. It includes those relationships with people you do *not* know personally. In the **D** ring are strangers on buses, store clerks, waiters, waitresses, the person seated next to you at lectures, meetings, or doctors' offices; it includes gas-station attendants, movie stars, ushers, cabdrivers, postal clerks, librarians—anyone you encounter in life briefly. They are not acquaintances or friends.

These people are not ones you necessarily confide in or expect deep and meaningful exchange of heart and soul with.

One day when I was shopping in a grocery store in New York City with my daughter, who was then about four years old, a woman turned around in the checkout line and began a conversation. She didn't talk to me, she talked to my little girl. She poured out her heart to the amazed child in about four minutes' time. She told her about her health, her husband's health, her pills, the liver ailment which had recently taken her sister's life, and if I hadn't interrupted, she would have given the details of the funeral. This is an excellent example of ill placement of confidence.

Sometimes I'll hear people say, "Oh, they're so unfriendly at that store," or "I don't like to eat at that restaurant because the waiters are so cold," or "The people in that town aren't outgoing!"

You will spare yourself a lot of disappointment and hurt if you stop expecting strangers to treat you like a friend. If it's a friend you want to talk to, call up somebody you know. If it's counseling you want, call your pastor or a professional Christian therapist. There are also loving, caring Christians who would count it a privilege to love you. A stranger can't give you what these people can.

If it's love you want, don't seek it where you won't find it (and that means your dentist, bus driver, podiatrist, and real-estate agent!). You need a Christian friend if you want love. Your **D** relationships are usually business; they're cordial (if possible) and distant. Your human worth does not depend upon responses of these people to you. They don't know you and are not personally involved with you. So the next time a waiter is surly to you, you can smile confidently and tell yourself, *Praise God, my personhood does not depend upon whether or not a stranger is polite to me.* Then, since you may be the only one to bless that person all day, you can say a quiet prayer for him or her and enjoy your meal.

Knowing who **D** relationships are in your life should make you sensitive to others who do not know this differentiation. When a stranger tells you his or her problems on the bus, you can be kind and understanding, knowing he needs something you are unable to give, but you can care and pray for him at that moment. It could help him and even change his life.

Countless times I am met by strangers who will pour out hurts and problems, even weep in deepest distress. Not long ago I was out jogging when I heard a woman sobbing. I followed the sounds until I came upon a woman utterly bound in grief over the loss of her husband. She was sitting in her garage. I prayed for her and became her friend in that moment of intense need.

Many times on airplanes I listen to life stories of strangers who are hurting. For those hours we are friends. I have given away books, sent Christian materials later, and given referrals of churches and people who could be of further help. Some of these people have kept in contact over the years, but usually once the plane lands, we disappear from one another into the crowds of other strangers, and the moments we shared become memories.

I'm talking about giving, not expecting to receive. Loved Persons are givers. In giving, you get back more than you ever could ask for. Every person you meet is a potential friend.

If you are a pastor, Bible teacher, Christian worker, or minister, you can expect people to come to you with their hurts and needs whether or not they know you. They will come to you in restaurants, airports, shopping centers, corridors, jogging trails—wherever you are, they will find you. These moments are precious. Your life touches someone else's and, in a wonderful, mysterious way, you are united for that moment in giving, selfless love.

2. *The C Ring:* The people in this ring are those whose lives often cross yours, such as people in church, your hairdresser or barber, people at work or school, fellow car poolers, neighbors, most people on your Christmas card list, distant relatives, committee members, the guys at the gym or the gals at the spa, your children's teachers; in other words, the people you have occasion to see or come in contact with fairly often, but whom you are *not* close friends with.

These are the people you chat with, engage in friendly conversation with, but they are not close friends now. It would be out of place to confide your hidden secrets to your son's baseball coach. It would be out of place to call your mailman and ask his advice on whether or not to dedicate your life to foreign missions.

The people in the C ring are people whom you care about, but who are not major characters in the scenario of your life. The relationships you have with people in this ring are almost always friendly and cordial. They are the people at church you see every week; they may be other parents at P.T.A. meetings, and you more than probably like them. They also like you, although they are not obligated to. You are committed to the people on this level only as far as your common interests extend. There is not a commitment on a close-friendship level, although these relationships could develop into closer ones. As a closer relationship forms, it would move into the B ring.

3. *The B Ring:* Herein are the true friends you care about and who care about you. A friend in this ring is one who

cries when you do, laughs when you do, and who considers you an important person to him or her. The **B** ring friends are not your closest, most intimate friends, but these are friends you genuinely enjoy and want to keep. You have a commitment with these friends. You've shown your love and concern and they've proven their friendship to you. A friend in this ring can usually be trusted with your secrets. You can call upon them in need and they can call upon you in need, too.

These are people you share the personal things in your life with (and not with the stewardess, the tour guide, or your swimming instructor). If you will see your relationships in their proper present order, you will save yourself a lot of heartache, hurt, and confusion.

A student of mine called me one night when I was fast asleep and told me, "Marie, you're the only person I can talk to."

It was 3:00 A.M.

He said, "You're the only person in the world who understands me."

I asked who was calling.

He told me his name. I had only seen him twice and at that, with a hundred other students. I told him I would be glad to understand him in the morning, but if it was at all possible, right then I wanted to sleep.

"Oh, it can't wait," he protested. "I have to talk to you right now!"

I convinced him in as kind a manner as possible to call me in the morning so I could arrange to see him about his problem. He obliged, and the next morning he showed up at my office. His problem? Insomnia.

This student felt no hesitancy to call at 3:00 A.M. because he did not see his teacher as someone fitting the **D** ring description—he saw me as a friend, someone who would help at any hour. Ideally these choices are come upon by two people and, by and large, friends are quite considerate of each other, only disturbing privacy in times of greatest urgency. Most people in helping professions, such as teachers, therapists, pastors, and doctors, make it known when they are accessible. These people are not strangers because they're there to help you. They should fit in your **B** category for as long as you need them there.

People in the **B** ring can include the friends in your prayer group or your therapy group. These are relationships that began in the **C** ring and moved into **B**. I have seen many wonderful fellowships develop through group therapy, prayer fellowships, and care groups. These friends are also your church family, but the relationships are *developed.* Just because you are brothers and sisters in the Lord, bound together in His love, don't expect every Christian to be your close friend and committed to you personally.

If you don't understand this, you can be easily hurt. A Christian brother and sister who unwittingly don't respond to you the way you want them to will appear to you as cold, unfriendly, or unloving. They may be people in the **D** or **C** ring of your present relationships and you are expecting them to be as involved with your life as a **B** relationship friend would be.

4. *The A Ring:* These are your closest, most intimate friends. This is where your husband or wife belongs. Most people do not have many people in this ring because of the deep commitment involved. An **A** ring relationship isn't with a faraway person or relative who calls once a month on the telephone. You may have many friends or relatives in other states whom you love dearly, but your **A** relationship is with a person who shares your everyday life.

Don't confuse an **A** friend with someone who belongs in the **B** category. You are not married to your best friend who moved to Walla Walla. He or she is a wonderful friend, but is not currently sharing your daily life.

Your children can be in this **A** category if you let them. Your children can be your dearest, most treasured friends. Your mother or father can be in this category, too. So can your brother or sister, aunt or cousin.

The person or persons in your **A** ring are the one(s) to whom you give your heart as fully as is humanly possible. Here is where you lay your life down for another person. Your deepest passion is for his or her very best. You cherish this one, love him or her so completely that God is able to express His abiding love through you to them. You love your husband or wife body, soul, and spirit. There is nothing that can hinder your love for your beloved because you refuse to love less than wholly.

An example of **A** devotion is a statement made by D. L. Moody's niece about the great evangelist and his wife, Emma Revell Moody: "Aunt Emma and Uncle Dwight were so perfectly one that nobody could possibly tell which was the one."

An **A** relationship is one where you are free to be yourself at all times because you are accepted without reservation. With this special person, you do not have to work at impressing. You are free to make mistakes, free from pretenses, free to be wonderful or not so wonderful. You're applauded and appreciated even when you lose at something.

You may only have one or two **A** relationships in your entire life. Jesus, who is Lord of all relationships, is your Lover and Best Friend, and He fits perfectly in your **A** ring. He is always there.

To sum up the relationship rings, they are:

D for strangers
C for casual relationships
B for close friends
A for your intimate and closest relationships

Your life is well balanced when you have people in every ring. (The only exception is **A**. It has fewer people than the other rings and it is possible not to have anyone except Jesus in that ring.)

Sometimes the friends we have in the **B** category stay in the **B** category, never becoming **A** friends. An **A** friend is one who shares your joy, hurt, good, and not so good.

> Human beings deserve to be loved by other human beings, and that includes appreciation and respect, even when we aren't altogether lovely.

An example of this priceless relationship is described by the poet Algernon Swinburne in his poem "A Match":

> If love were what the rose is,
> And I were like the leaf,
> Our lives would grow together
> In sad or singing weather.

Love won't fade out or become obsolete or come to a dead end if you take care of it. The Loved Person is a lover and a giver in all relationships.

yanked by truth

my soul was in misbelief prison
    all afternoon
as i fed on the bread
    of hurt feelings.
hurt and imprisoned,
    my heart held no
banners of love, joy;
    least of all PEAce
,and i sat smack
    inthemiddleofa
wet
      cold
      dappled
      cloud.
i called out to God
    to yank my soul
    out of prison
and it was not long
      before
i heard, "Let not your
    heart be TROUBLED"
,sharp as a blade zinging
    through the air
    on its way to my brain
,cutting through sin
    slicing
the lies &
    misbeliefs
(such as:
  Everyone Should
  Love Me)
to bits

14

The Loveless Habit of Jealousy

I want to discuss a ferocious enemy of love: jealousy. This sin sneaks among the people of God like a worm after the sweetest part of the fruit. It is a killer.

Here we are, imagine now, standing out in a playground. Near us are two children who have only one toy between them. They both want it. There is a foray for the toy and one child wins, the other loses. The child who loses pulls back with tightened muscles. His heart races, his fists are clenched. He copes with the situation the only way he knows how. "I hate you!" he shouts tearfully.

Adults do the same, only not quite so overtly. Perhaps it would be better to face the person you're jealous of and openly declare, "I am jealous of you and that is why I behave the unpleasant way I do. You have something I want and because I have inappropriate coping skills, I can only fight back by hating you and trying to hurt you."

Instead, most adults experience their jealousy in secret, and the war they wage is far more venomous than even they suspect. Nobody wins.

Why You Become Jealous

Let's look at the case of Tom D., a young pastor in a growing church in the middle of a large city. He claims he is a man of love and mercy. If you could hear him put down some famous ministers, however, you'd sure think he misunderstood the word *mercy.* In Tom's opinion, nearly every large Christian ministry is off the beam and all wrong in their evangelistic tactics and practices. Tom's ministry, of course, is the one that is practically perfect in all aspects of it. Tom thinks his views show "discernment." God calls it jealousy.

Another person is Talbot, a medical student, who studies long, hard hours. School is not easy for him and he works faithfully and diligently in preparation for all his work, but especially hard during exams. Fred, his friend, seems to breeze through his classes and tests and receives better grades than Talbot. Seething, Talbot starts a rumor that Fred is cheating.

Then there's Clara, whose husband offers a hand of kindness to the widow across the street by repairing her car. Because the widow is attractive, Clara insults her husband with hurtful and cutting remarks. Had the widow been an old homely woman, perhaps Clara wouldn't have minded his helping her.

What do you see in these examples? Let me put it another way. What *don't* you see?

You don't see love, do you? Let me qualify that. There are two kinds of love we are capable of. One is human, or natural love. The other is supernatural, or God's love. This last one is the agape love this book is primarily centered on.

This *highest* love is altogether too rare to find at times. Our own natural affections and feelings are what we may call human love. With our human love we can do lots of noble things. In fact, Jesus told us that human love can really be pretty terrific. "Greater love hath no man than this, that a man lay down his life for his friends," He said (John 15:13). Lots of people have laid down their lives for somebody else. Look at the number of soldiers who have died in wars for nameless, faceless countrymen they didn't even know. The selfless, higher love of God gives us courage to be and act in ways far greater than our own human abilities allow. We become magnificently giving because He is love. His love transcends evil.

Human affection won't suffice because we need a sacrificial element that goes beyond our human capability if we are to understand love. "... while we were yet *sinners,* Christ died for us" (Romans 5:8, my italics) is an incredible and astounding act of love. This is the same love that lives in you. Jesus not only laid down His life for His friends but He laid it down for His enemies as well. Human love is incapable of doing that.

In order for you to overcome jealousy, you take His divine love as a characteristic of your own personality and being. Jesus has made you one with Him. You have the power to rise above your own human powers.

Love is sometimes so odd to us, so weird, so unlike anything realistic, that we cannot grasp it. *"What?"* cries Clara. "You mean I should encourage my husband to help that woman? Have you *seen* her?"

Yes, help her. Love her as Jesus loves her. Give of yourself. Give, and then thank God that you can give of your love without holding back, without strife, without jealousy.

Love was so amazing and incomprehensible in the person of Jesus that the Prophet Isaiah prophesied of His divine act, "... he hath no form nor comeliness; and when we shall see him, there is no beauty that we should desire him" (Isaiah 53:2). God laid down His life for His *enemies* as well as His

friends, and in the light of such sublime love, we're awed.
Clara suffers jealousy because she believes:

1. I am only worthy until someone worthier comes along.
2. I must constantly be in control of everything that belongs to me.
3. The love and devotion of my spouse is the most important thing in my life.
4. Anything that gains the interest of my spouse is a threat to his devotion to me.
5. To be inferior to anything or anyone is awful.
6. I am a person who is not worthy of faithful love from another.

This is only one of many jealous incidents in Clara's life. At the age of forty-seven, she has nearly destroyed her entire family with her behavior.

Clara came for counseling when she saw the problems she was causing. Closely related to her jealous feelings was the overwhelming controlling urge we talked about earlier. Her feelings of inadequacy were most painful. One day she made a wonderful realization which she shared with me: "Marie, I have gone to church most of my life and I never even thought about living in the love of God. My concept of love has always been—well, as you say, just *human*. But I want to change. I *want* to enter into the love of the Lord."

Clara did change. She worked on her thoughts and the information she pumped into her belief system. She told herself every day the sentences I've outlined for you in this book. At first she rebelled against anything that took the least bit of extra effort. But finally, she accepted the fact that her behavior was due to her wrong beliefs. Her mistaken self-talk had to be replaced with truth.

Talbot was a fellow who had to learn a new set of sentences to tell himself, also. His story could have ended in despair. He was apprehended by the dean of his college and put on probation because of the conflict he had stirred up. Instead of getting Fred into trouble, which had been his intention, he got himself into trouble. It worked out for the good of him, though, because he was forced to get help and work on his problem.

"I'm a Christian," he confessed ashamedly. "How could I do something so evil? I could have ruined Fred's entire career."

Tom believed erroneously:

1. My achievements are not important unless they're more or better than someone else's.
2. I am only worthy if I compare favorably to others.
3. To fail when others succeed is unfair.
4. I am a failure until I prove otherwise.
5. To lose something valuable is the worst thing on earth.
6. All men are created equal, so I should have what others have.

As long as Tom continued with these wrong beliefs, he would not live in victory. As long as he continued to put down other ministries and other people, he could not live in love. Without love we fail, because the only thing that doesn't fail is love.

The Answer to Jealousy

You are capable of human love. Anybody is. You can love a person, an ideology—in fact, a myriad of things. You can be passionately devoted to a philosophy, political system, a person—even lay down your life for them. But God is seeking your supernatural Christian love-self, which is higher than human devotion. God's eyes go to and fro throughout the earth looking for someone He can be Himself through, someone who will love beyond human power or ability.

As a Christian, not only can I lay down my life for you but I can also love you while doing it. I can forgive while doing it. I can sacrifice all for you because your greater good is of urgent importance to me.

Because I want more than anything in this life to see you rise to great heights in God, I want you to know Him as He is, in His love for you. There is no victory in your life I will fail to celebrate. There is no breath of my own life I would not give for your victory.

First: Combat the enemies of God by making a commitment to the Word of God. You *decide* openly, consciously, actively, forthright and boldly, that you are going to agree with what the Word says. You tell yourself, *I will be a doer and not just a hearer.*

Love is action, yes. But what prompts the action? What trains you for action? *Your words.* Your self-talk is utterly vital to your happiness or unhappiness. Are you speaking the words God has spoken to us through His Word? Or are you speaking a pack of world-influenced nonsense?

God and His Word are one. What God *says* is who God *is.* You must learn His Words in order to learn His heart.

Second: Let's *apply* the truths of God to everyday life. Tell yourself loud and clear, in a voice you can hear, what Clara, Talbot, and Tom had to:

1. I am not a jealous person.
2. I refuse jealousy in any form.
3. I am totally in love with God and I trust His judgment.
4. I willingly give all that I am to God.
5. Nobody can take anything from me, for I already lay claim to no thing but God and His love for me.
6. I stand against jealousy in the name of Jesus.

7. I choose to love all people.
8. I choose to seek others' higher good.
9. I choose to devote my life to seeing that others become all they can be in Jesus.
10. I relinquish control of my life, job, and family, to God and the power of His love.
11. It's okay with me if others have more than I.
12. I am a person worthy of love and I accept that love.
13. I am a Loved Person. I am jealous of no one on earth.

Jealousy is a putrid offense. When you see your brother or sister owning the very gift you desire and do not have, you can throw a party in your heart, rejoicing and surprising yourself with words such as, "Thank You, Jesus! That person exceeds me!"

The Loved Person is at one with God, at peace, and completely satisfied in the knowledge of God and His personhood. He does not want. You may say to me at this juncture, "Oh, Marie, isn't that a little *too* altruistic? How can anyone be *that* unselfish?" That's just *it!* You and I really can't be, unless we're being phonies, manipulators, or masochists. This is what I'm talking about when I say God wants us to love with *supernatural* love.

I don't think, in my own human affection, I can rejoice freely when somebody else wins the prize I've longed for and worked for; or when somebody else has the answers to all my goals and dreams while I'm left lacking. No, I think I'd be green with jealousy and anger. I would think it unfair. I might even think God Himself was unfair.

Praise God, Loved Person, we're above that now. We can truly smile toward heaven and say to the Lord, "It is well with my soul. I know You will always prosper me and You will always shine Your blessings upon me. I am jealous of no person on earth."

When you have prayed for a certain thing and you are denied it for the time being for some reason known only to God, you can rest with ecstasy in your soul no less than when you receive the answer. Then when you spot someone else (whom you think is perhaps not as worthy as you) with your treasure, you are prepared to rejoice with him or her and thank God for blessing him so wonderfully.

These words I'm telling you are not options, they're orders. ". . . jealousy is cruel as the grave . . ." it says in Song of Solomon 8:6. ". . . the coals thereof are coals of fire, which hath a most vehement flame." Is that any way to live?

"Jealousy is the rage of a man . . ." we read in the Book of Proverbs (6:34). God tells us to be like *Him.* He doesn't give us a list of nice thoughts as options and then tell us to pick and choose which one might fit in with our life-style. He tells us outright, "By this we know that we have come to know Him, if we keep His commandments. The one who says, 'I have come to know Him,' and does not keep His commandments, is a liar, and the truth is not in him" (1 John 2:3, 4 NAS).

In practical terms, He is teaching us to remove jealousy from our hearts and to "walk in the same manner as He walked" (1 John 2:6 NAS).

> The only One we know who can get away with being jealous is the Lord Himself. He can't stand it when we don't behave in love.

We have to be careful we don't go against God's law of love and mercy. The place where you are utterly safe is tucked snugly in His heart of love. It's the heart of Jesus that pleases the Father, and it's there you're happiest. Jesus said that He always does what pleases the Father (John 8:29). When you are one with His Spirit, He does what pleases God

through you! In that place of safety, you lose the habit of
jealousy that you made yourself miserable with. You're
free—free to love and be loved wholly.

> **free**
>
> free, Lord,
> i'm free
> ,free from the fairgrounds
> and circuses of attention
> seeking
> ,and free from popping in the thin skin
> of prestige grabbing
> .free
> from practicing how to be
>   religious
> ,free
> from tallying good works
> like home runs on a scoresheet
> ,free
> to help others without
> talking about it
> ,free
> to be
> quiet
> ,to be
> unvarnished
> ,to be in love
> with You
> because You
>   love me
> . the sour taste of
> strife is gone
>   and love
>   has made me
>   free
>   from my ominous
>   enemy,
> me.

15

Say Good-bye to Worry

Let me introduce Donna to you. As a child, Donna was a "model daughter." Her sister, a year older, who had been adored by the family and all who knew her, had died at the age of seven. Donna felt it really should have been she who died because she wasn't half as good or as pretty as her sister. In order to justify her life, she became the nicest, sweetest girl she could be. She worked hard in school, got good grades, kept herself clean, acted politely always, and tried never to cause her parents any problems. She got the reputation for being a wonderful, sweet, thoughtful, courteous girl. She worried terribly that she'd lose her parents' love if she were ever to disappoint them by letting them see she really wasn't what she appeared to be.

When she was older, she continued to meet the expectations of others and earn the right to exist by becoming the model wife. Her husband raved at the wonderful housekeeper she was and expected her to stay the giving, selfless person he thought she was.

In reality, Donna was wearing thin with her playing up to others' expectations. She worried constantly. She really didn't always feel as sweet as she pretended she was. What if someone were to find out? She worried she'd lose everything.

Secretly she fantasized that some low-life rogue would

find her and she'd be helpless to his foul insistence. Off she'd run to the wilds of debauchery with him. Then everyone would see the tough broad she feared she really was. Nobody suspected anything was wrong, even when she began drinking and was heard cursing. (Such a nice girl! Cursing?) Her husband figured it was because she was bored. So he suggested they start a family.

Three children later, Donna was still playing the role of the sweet pacifist, but continuing to hate and distrust herself. She overate in an attempt to prove how ugly she really was, and became fat as well as an alcoholic. Now she worried she had lost her looks.

Donna's worries were destroying her. In time her marriage ended in divorce and her husband gained custody of the children. He remarried two years later and Donna was sent to a state institution where her story could have ended, but one day a minister came to her room and told her about Jesus. She became a Christian and within months, was moved to a Christian halfway house for ex-alcoholics. She is there now as this book is being written. She is learning about God's love for her. She is learning about forgiveness. She is becoming aware that she is a Loved Person and that her worries are His now because she is His person. It's not easy for Donna, but she is learning to be free to be herself. She is discovering through the Lord just who that person is.

Donna wasted forty-two years of her life because of worry. I can't help thinking of Saint Francis' soul-stirring words when he gave his life to God after living so many years without Him: "Too late I have loved Thee, too late ..." he said. What a tragedy to wait so long before giving one's life to God. Saint Francis, in deepest love, made up for those lost years.

True love says, "I love you through thick and thin. You

deserve to live and be loved because you're you, not because you're nice. I love you when you are not perfect and when you are unlovely. It is not necessary for you to earn my love. It would hurt me to think you worried about earning my love. My love is free, without contingencies. It is unconditional. I love you because you *are*. Period."

Do you allow your worries to separate you from God?

Some of the most common worries are:

- money and the lack of it
- health
- not meeting others' expectations
- losing something precious or important
- the past
- the future

Notice that most of these worries center around *loss*. You can't lose Jesus. Because He's yours forever, you're safe. If you have Him you have all things. You know how to receive your blessings from Him. You know He loves you and is watching over you. You know how to *claim* what's yours as a Christian.

Worry will not hold a prominent position in your life when you learn how to pray for results. The first thing to know is that God *hears*. Remember, He and His Word are one. You have the privilege of knowing God's heart and will by knowing His Word. You can know His purposes and intentions for you and your life, and then pray them into existence.

Napoleon could have taken his own advice when he said, "The only conquests which are permanent, and leave no regrets, are our conquests over ourselves." Conquer your worries and you'll be mightier than a thousand armies.

Let's take each of the most common worries individually

and see how the power of love combats their lethal effects over you.

Worry About Money

Times are getting harder. You had better know how to stand on the Word of God for your needs. Answers don't just appear suddenly out of thin air because you have a problem. Faith is a gift God gives you because He loves you. You're the one who develops it.

You use your faith by standing on the Word of God regarding your needs. Do you have financial need? Don't lose your answers by choosing worry over faith in Jesus. You prosper as your soul (intellect, emotions, and will) prospers. You can ruin God's plan by starving your soul with doubting, fretting, and worrying.

God has some rules for prosperity, as with everything else. It's His blueprint and He expects us to follow it in order to reap the benefits which are rightfully ours as His children. Make this checklist for yourself:

1. Have I scrupulously tithed to God's work in order to keep God's order of prosperity, as in Leviticus 27:30–32? "Thus all the tithe of the land, of the seed of the land or of the fruit of the tree, is the Lord's; it is holy to the Lord. . . . And for every tenth part of herd or flock, whatever passes under the rod, the tenth one shall be holy to the Lord" (NAS).
2. Do I refuse to gain wealth by ungodly practices? "How blessed is the man who does not walk in the counsel of the wicked, Nor stand in the path of sinners, Nor sit in the seat of scoffers!" (Psalms 1:1 NAS).
3. Do I choose to trust God in *every* circumstance in my life? "They that trust in the Lord shall be as mount Zion, which cannot be removed, but abideth for ever" (Psalms 125:1).
4. Do I give freely of myself, my goods, my money, and my

love, so that I may reap back the same things I sow? "Be
not deceived; God is not mocked: for whatsoever a man
soweth, that shall he also reap" (Galatians 6:7).

5. Do I place the uncompromised Word of God *first* in my
life, refusing to doubt that He truly loves and watches over
me? "Thy word have I treasured in my heart, That I may
not sin against Thee" (Psalms 119:11 NAS). ". . . whoso
putteth his trust in the Lord shall be safe" (Proverbs 29:25).

6. Have I walked in love? "And walk in love, as Christ also
hath loved us, and hath given himself for us . . ." (Ephesians 5:2).

Pray with me: *Father in the name of Jesus, I will not give
any part of myself over to worry. I choose to believe your
promise that I will prosper as my soul prospers. I refuse
Satan's lies and threats of defeat. I trust You, Jesus!*

Worry About Health

Love covers your health needs. God loves your body.
Jesus died so that you can be forgiven of your sins and made
alive and new in every area of your life.

- Stand on the promise of God that says, ". . . with his stripes
we are healed" (Isaiah 53:5).
- Stand on the promise, ". . . I am the Lord that healeth thee"
(Exodus 15:26).
- Stand on the promise that God will protect and keep you in
all your ways, including health. "The Lord will keep you
from all evil; He will keep your life. The Lord will keep
your going out and your coming in from this time forth and
for evermore" (Psalms 121:7, 8 AMPLIFIED).
- Stand on the promise that God designed and loves your
body as well as the rest of you. He wants you alive and well.
"He sends forth His word and heals them and rescues them
from the pit and destruction" (Psalms 107:20 AMPLIFIED).
- Stand on the promise that love is not impatient. Even if you
don't get an answer immediately, love never fails, and you

can be patient and continue to stand in faith through thick and thin, trusting God and refusing to worry. "Dwell in Me and I will dwell in you.—Live in Me and I will live in you . . ." (John 15:4 AMPLIFIED).

> Behold, God is my salvation,
> I will trust and not be afraid;
> For the Lord God is my strength and song,
> And He has become my salvation."
>
> Isaiah 12:2 NAS

Pray with me: *Lord Jesus, I know that by Your stripes I am healed and can stay healed. I refuse to worry. Thank You, Lord!*

Worry About Others' Expectations of You

You are you. You are not an object. For a long time in my own life, I must confess, I went after the approval of others before even considering what God had to say. People expected me to be on top of things, to be strong and helpful at all times, and so I felt obligated to live up to those expectations, but honestly, sometimes I would not be on top of things. I wouldn't have answers. It was at those times I'd be tempted to feel inadequate, as if I had failed somehow. This reaction, God tells us, is just plain *sin.*

I've learned, through His grace, that the expectations we have to meet are *His.* If we please God, we don't ever have to worry about pleasing people. I may not meet your expectations, but I promise I will be faithful to God and I will live consecrated to this pledge to Him with all my soul, body, and spirit. If I do not please you, forgive me. I'd prefer it if I met your expectations of me and that I had your approval, but if it's not possible, I want you to know I'll not manipulate, work overtime, or strive in any way for it. I give you the right to your feelings and opinions. I also give myself the right to live irrespective of your approval.

When we are locked in God's love, living within the law of love, our minds totally made up to follow love, we can say to one another, "I love you, not because you love me, but because I choose to see you as valuable and important. Together we belong to God."

Your self-talk is vital. Check yourself. What are the words you're currently telling yourself? Do you hear yourself speaking worrisome self-talk like the following?

- So-and-so doesn't like me. I just can't understand why.
- What if I'm not really as clever as my teacher thinks I am?
- If I don't do exactly as others expect of me, I may lose their friendship. That would be terrible.
- I wouldn't dare let anyone see me looking bad.
- I must always be cheerful and outgoing because that's what people expect of Christians.
- I can't let anybody know that I am not Mr. (Mrs.) Perfecto.
- I never have any time (money, rewards) for myself. All I do is serve others. People expect it of me. What can I do?

I am sure you can add several of your own sentences to the above. It's possible for you to be manipulated to become what another person *expects* instead of who you really *are.* In order to resist this temptation to live up to all expectations, you need a clear picture of what love is. Love is strong. Love is wise. Jesus was no pushover. He was love, but He wasn't a giddy heart ready to jump every time somebody snapped his or her fingers. *Jesus could not be manipulated.* He didn't worry about anybody's expectations of Him. If He had, He never would have gone to the cross. He would have wanted to look like the hero His disciples saw Him as.

How disappointed they were when they saw Him hanging on the cross, naked and broken, no better than a common thief! Jesus *knew* what He was doing; He knew *who* He was and *why* He had to die. "I go to prepare a place for you. . . . I will send you another Comforter [the Holy Spirit]. . . . For this is My blood of the new testament, which is shed for many for the remission of sins. . . . Yet a little while I am with you, and then I go to Him that sent Me. . . . If I be lifted up, I will draw all men unto Me. . . ."

Tell yourself true statements instead of ones that manipulate you into being someone you really aren't.

Say out loud:

- I will not try to be someone I am not in order to fulfill someone else's expectations.
- I am precious to God and I refuse to worry about whether or not I meet people's expectations.
- I am a person with pluses as well as minuses. I accept both the pluses and the minuses, and I will not lie to others or myself about them.
- I am a lovable Christian person, and most people will accept me for who I am.

Donna, the lady I told you about at the beginning of this chapter, lamented all the years she had wasted worrying about whether or not she was pleasing people. "I was trapped," she told her prayer group. "But now that I've gotten a glimpse of freedom from those fears and worries, I'll never go back. No, never."

Neither will you. I have confidence in you. If Donna can find freedom through the cross of Christ, if I can, if multitudes of others can, so can you! We're not losers. And that brings us to the next popular worry: the worry about losing something or someone.

Worry About Losing Someone or Something

Love covers loss. You don't lose with God. You only gain. Even when you think you've lost, you haven't. "It is your Father's good pleasure to give you the kingdom," Jesus told us (Luke 12:32). Love is a giver.

In God's Kingdom, loss becomes profit. He turns every lack and what we call loss into something glorious for us and for Himself.

As His child:

You do not lose honor.
You do not lose prestige.
You do not lose face.
You do not lose love.

The only way you hinder God's principle of gain is to worry. You worry anxiously when there's nothing to worry about. ("Why is my husband fixing that woman's car? Is it because she's young and pretty? Maybe I'll lose him to someone pretty like that one day.")

A child worries about losing a friend because he or she goes on vacation and leaves for an extended time. A man nearing retirement age worries a younger man might snatch his job out from under him. A fashion model worries about losing her looks. Loss, loss, loss.

The primary misbelief is, "I cannot lose anything. To lose something or someone is terrible, awful, dreadful! I couldn't stand that."

Bold-faced lies. *Of course,* you can lose something. You can lose your job, friends, money, prestige, reputation, husband, wife, even a part of your body—and you can go on living triumphantly and happily. It's ridiculous to think you can't lose. Many of us have lost things that were precious to us, and we are not moping or living deprived lives.

Say out loud several times a day, "I'm not a loser. I'm a winner. God doesn't destroy His children. God is a giver. He *keeps* that which is His. What I consider loss is really gain."

Worry About the Past

Love covers the past. It's over now. You are not your past. You are your *now*. Your sins are forgiven; your wounds are healed. Your joys are past joys and are now memories to be cherished, but not enslaved to. Your eyes are opened. Yesterday may have been beautiful or horrendous, but you're alive *today* and it's the only today you've got.

- You can change old habits of the past. Instead of worrying, you can change.
- You can insist others release themselves from the past, too. Life is *now*.
- It is *not* true that all you are today is due to your past experiences. You choose to respond to and interpret past events, circumstances, and relationships according to your *now* thinking. A thing is only as bad or as good as you tell yourself it is.

If you are in bondage to the past, you may be teaching yourself to:

- stay lonely
- feel condemned and guilty when there's no need to
- avoid accepting *now* challenges to enter new experiences
- be suspicious about anything regarding risk, including making new friends, changing jobs, dating, or even making a commitment to one church by joining it for better or worse

- stay trapped in old negative thought patterns and refuse inner growth
- choose immobilization over disapproval or failure

Allow the past to be a blessing to you. Say, "Past of mine, I bless you in the name of Jesus. When I ask God for forgiveness, He gives it to me. Now I forgive myself, too. It's over and gone. I am a brand-new person, separate and wonderfully alive! As wonderful, also, as the past may have been, I look forward to an even more wonderful future."

That means looking forward to the future, not worrying about it. Unfortunately, it's a very popular worry. Let's discuss it a little bit before I end this chapter.

Worry About the Future

Jesus holds you in the palm of His hand. You are the apple of God's eye. He tenderly watches over you so no harm can come your way. He blesses you with long life and good things. In this life and after it you belong to God. Mercy and love are your friends and your allies.

That which you fear will more than likely never happen. Besides, it's a misbelief that you can't handle problems that may come your way.

"Oh, the economy is so terrible!" I overheard in the church lobby.

"I know!" was the reply. "Isn't it *awful?* Do you know that eggs cost six times what they used to?"

"Isn't it *awful?* I don't know what this world is coming to."

"We're near the end. I don't know what we'll all do. We already are having a rough time making ends meet."

"Isn't it *awful!*"

I must answer that last exclamation with a *no!* It *isn't* awful. Praise God, these things give us an opportunity to exercise our faith, take hold of our Talent, pray and stand fast on the Word of God, then watch God prove Himself. Accept hardship as a challenge to prove God is who He says He is.

Daniel Webster once said, "The most important thought I ever had was that of my individual responsibility to God." Interesting, isn't it? One of the greatest minds ever, and he talked about *God* being his most important thought. Our responsibility to God is to take Him at His word. He says to fret not, to trust Him, to take up our cross and follow Him, to love and be loved.

Our future is assured in Christ. He is our Shepherd, we shall not want. We will not fear for one single moment about what the future may look like. We know, because we belong to Jesus, it will be good.

Pray with me: *Lord, I believe in You. When I haven't faith, I have to have faith in Your faith. You believe in me. You see my future filled with promise. I will choose to see as You see, with hope and with fearlessness.*

As E. Stanley Jones said: "Repeat to your soul these words: 'To say what ought to be cannot be is a brief and complete statement of atheism.' It is. Say to yourself, 'What ought to be can be, and I will make it so.' And you will. You will go beyond yourself."

Your future is bright and filled with promises to bring glory to God. Going beyond yourself, you can discard your worries forever.

a fresh start

this is thanks
for all things new
,Lord. new and clean.
i will bless and love
You
for what i've seen,
the victories i've
          celebrated
                    because
                    of
                    You
,and now because we love
          each other
i've become the w
                    e
                         a
                         k
          made strong

16

Loving Him Back: A Final Word

A couple of days ago my telephone rang and the woman on the other end of the wire told me, "Marie, my life will never be the same since I realized how much the Lord loves me. I feel as though the whole world has opened up to me and I can now go forward as a true child of God!"

I feel the same way as that woman. The realization of God's love has revolutionized my life. I had been a Christian since I was a young child; I had taught Sunday school, been a junior church director, gone to Bible college, led Bible classes, written books, and served God for at least ten years, and then it hit me—*God loves me!*

I knew all the Bible verses about love. I could quote them in my sleep. I had even taught an entire semester on 1 Corinthians 13. But when I committed myself to what I have shared with you in this book, I gained something inwardly that I never had before. I've seen the same transformation that happened to me take place in the lives of countless others during the last six years of teaching *Love and Be Loved* principles.

But the reason for this transformation is not just the realization of being loved by God—it is also loving Him back.

It is not possible to love Him from a truly holy heart without knowing His immense love for us first. "We love him, because he first loved us" (1 John 4:19) is the first principle which takes root as a reality in our lives.

I meet dozens of Christians who want to serve God, want to beat paths on foreign soil, want to herald the formation of a new church, want to be apostles, prophets, pastors, evangelists; they want to get out there in the sin-sick jungle of the world and do great things for God.

Let me tell you, many men and women with evangelistic zeal have plunged ahead to serve God, and zeal being their main motivator, they've failed. You don't do great things for God without what we have discussed in this book. It's impossible! No matter what you do, it won't mean two beans in the Kingdom of God. "He that loveth not knoweth not God; for God is love" (1 John 4:8).

Loved Persons can sacrifice, deny themselves, suffer peril, and never be impatient with God. Loved Persons can experience trouble, lack, and want without thinking they're out of the will of God. Loved Persons know how to fight for what's theirs as children of the Kingdom. They don't give up. Nothing any person or demon of hell can do will defeat our Loved Person. You know *who* you are and the authority you have.

All that you have in Christ is still not as important as the main purpose for being and living as a Loved Person. Its main purpose is this: to love God in return.

The glory of your life is in loving God. When His love pours through your being, you find how capable you are of loving Him back. ". . . the love of God has been poured out within our hearts through the Holy Spirit who was given to us" (Romans 5:5 NAS).

Poured! Within! Love poured like hot metal to set within

you, unbreakable, unmovable, costly, and gorgeous. This love is not only external with blessings: it's *within*. Admit it. Face it. You're filled with love and will love God back *His* way.

Loving God

The Lord wants us to love Him His way. When you love God perfectly, you love Him with a loved heart. As with a friend, you're at home with Him. You're bold in your love, unafraid to approach Him, unashamed to drink in His Word night and day. The reason you are to get His love planted firmly within you is so that you can obey these words: "Thou shalt love the Lord thy God with all thine heart, and with all thy soul, and with all thy might" (Deuteronomy 6:5).

God tells us how to do that. You don't do it by running off to an underdeveloped country the week after you become a Christian to lead thousands of "savage heathens" to Christ. You're not grounded in *love* yet. The greatest of all virtues is love. You'll only come back home with a chip on your shoulder and angry at God for not making it easier for you to be a hero of the faith if you're not grounded in love.

Love is mature. The love of a baby for its parent is wonderful and gratifying, but the parent is in the position of protector, provider, and giver. As the child grows, a relationship develops between parent and child. Now the child says, "Thanks, Mom!" and "I love you, Dad!" and "I've got the best parents in the whole wide world!" because he has developed in love and can now express it. Later, his actions show his love, too.

God loves the nursery, but His best friends are those He can communicate with and whose actions reflect Himself.

One trait of a lover is that he isn't rude to his loved one. When you love God, you aren't rude to Him. You don't insult Him by blaming Him every time something goes wrong. You don't threaten Him when life isn't going your way with words such as, "God, why don't you *do* something?" Or, "How could *You* let this happen to me?"

I remember one day when I was leading group therapy, a man and a woman were talking together during the break. I was close by and observed the exchange between them. She had just accidentally spilled his coffee. It was all over his sleeve as well as his notebook and the table. He just grinned and helped mop it up. She said how sorry she was; he said it was nothing, he could have done it himself. Suddenly, they were giggling. The coffeepot was empty, so there was no more to replace what had been spilled, but he was jovial about it. She gave him her coffee. More giggles. They then shared her coffee and returned to the group grinning.

I was fascinated. They were falling in love! How did I know? One very telling observation: they enjoyed each other even when things went wrong.

Married people often cease to enjoy one another through bad times if one of them is the cause of the bad times. The Christian husband and wife may stick it out together through thick and thin, but *enjoy* each other?

Imagine the wife who is getting ready for a special event. She has packed the family station wagon up with picnic fixings and has things all in order for a gala family reunion. She had gotten the family up early because there'd be a five-hour drive and she knew her husband wanted to get there in plenty of time to set up the decorations and games. Into the station wagon they climb. The baby is strapped in his car seat, Junior and Sissy are buckled in their seats in the rear, and Fido, the dog, is curled up in the back with the blankets and extra clothes. Dad turns the ignition. No gas. How do you suppose the Mrs. will respond?

Or how about this? You're a hardworking man and you have put in a week of grueling overtime on the job. Your wife, who doesn't work, forgot to mail the house payment for last month and you're charged the twenty-five-dollar late fee. How are you going to mention this oversight to her?

Take little Junior, who has decided to teach Sissy the way a true artist would paint Fido's portrait. The only canvas available is the newly painted dining room wall, so there to greet Daddy's boss and wife at dinner a couple of hours later is a bigger-than-life-size rendering of something that looks like a cross between the Incredible Hulk and King Kong. Just how would *you* handle this little infraction? Will poor Junior be able to dine tonight in a sitting position?

Love is patient. How difficult it is to be patient when you're right and the other person is wrong! How justified you feel to be furious when you have been wronged. If somebody talks cruelly about you, you feel no remorse at cutting him down.

I'm not saying that the Loved Person is a pushover. May it never be said! You're not something of a clown, throwing candy kisses as you're being mowed down by villians. Love is wise.

Love is not only wise but it's kind as well. Love God with kindness. Be *kind* to God. Talk lovingly to Him, be thoughtful of Him, mindful of Him, consider *His* feelings and *His* wants.

Boldness vs. Pushiness

When you love God with patience and kindness, you aren't pushy. You're bold. Boldness and pushiness are two different things.

Pushiness says: "I come to the throne of grace because that's where the answers are given out. I want what I want and I'd better get it or else!"

Boldness says: "I come to the throne of grace because that's where my heart gets its life. I am God's property, a Loved Person, and I *know* my inheritance in Christ Jesus."

Satan wants you to worry more about yourself than to think about the Lord and His power and glory. Satan wants you to speculate and "tribulate." He wants you to fuss in your heart every time you see a younger Christian more successful than you. He wants you to distrust rich Christians, dislike those who reject you or hurt you, find fault with large ministries. Satan is the one who influences you to believe you must win every argument, be in control of other people's lives, envy, be jealous, strive for attention: win the approval of everybody around. Finally, one of Satan's worst tricks is to influence you so that you pray without faith or love. That way you won't please and bless the Lord.

Blessing the Lord

Bless the Lord, O my soul: and all that is within me, bless his holy name.

Psalms 103:1

Because you love Him, you will bless Him. *Tell* yourself to bless the Lord. Tell Him:

- Because I love You, I choose to be loving.
- Because I love You, I choose to be healthy.
- Because I love You, I choose to be happy.
- Because I love You, I choose to exercise self-control.
- Because I love You, I choose to stop grumbling.
- Because I love You, I will be jealous of no one.
- Because I love You, I am not a faultfinder, a backbiter, a

complainer, a gossiper, or a contender for approval—I'm a
Loved Person. *I love.*
- Because I love You, I will not be suspicious of other people.
- Because I love You, I will not try to control others' lives.

Now add your own "Because I love Him" sentences to the
list. Make some decisions about how you are going to bless
God with your life from now on.

It is wonderful to bless God with our joy, with our delight
in Him, with our health, our happiness, and our abundance.
We bless God by taking what Jesus did on the cross for us as
real.

The Cost of Loving God

Father Junípero Serra, who was one of the first mission-
aries to California, was martyred three hundred years ago in
front of the mission he had established in San Diego. Two of
his converts raised a rebellion and, with a band of other
hostile Indians, they charged the mission to "kill all the
white men." Fearlessly, Father Serra met them outside the
front door with his arms open in welcome as they advanced.
I visited the mission and saw the spot where they clubbed to
death this gentle, self-sacrificing man, and I was gripped
with emotion. His words as they charged him were, "Love
God, my children."

Do you really think you can be a follower of Christ without love? Do you really think you already know all there is
to know about love? I think once again of the life of Saint
Francis. He suffered many perils, and yet he never seemed
to lose his love. When his eyes had to be cauterized with a
red-hot iron, Saint Francis addressed fire as a brother and
requested that it cause him no pain. And he felt no pain as
his eyes were burned closed. At the hour of death he greeted

death as a sister, not an enemy. He transformed every experience to something loving.

You can give without loving but you can't love without giving.

You and I can change this world of ours by transforming every experience to something loving and good for God. We can take the most violent transgression, such as that committed against Father Serra, and transform it into a gift for God. We can take something frightening like fire and make it a friend—only by love.

Someone will inevitably say to me, "Oh, Marie, I don't need to hear a message about love. I know all about love. Besides that, my self-image is fine. I have a wonderful family who loves me."

Hitler and Mussolini were loved, too, believe it or not. Some of the most notorious criminals in history were loved by somebody or another. The love of God for you is entirely different from the love of a person. Being loved by someone (nonagape) is no feather in your cap. The song "You're Nobody 'til Somebody Loves You" just isn't true. You're somebody because the Big Somebody who matters loves you!

God will bless you with loved ones to cherish and love you, but remember, these loved ones only reflect a shadow of the magnitude of God's love for you. The admonition "Husbands, love your wives, even as Christ also loved the church . . ." (Ephesians 5:25) illustrates to us the immense value of His love as teacher, lover, protector, beautifier, and self-reinforcer. ". . . He that loveth his wife loveth *himself*" (verse 28, my italics). *God is love.*

Throughout this book I have shared with you how to live

the ultimate love experience every day of your life. I have wanted to be totally honest with you and strip away anything I have not proven to be real and true in my own life. I know without a shadow of a doubt that when you love God with all your heart, soul, and might, nothing is too hard for you.

I don't think of you as a stranger I've never met. I think of you as a Loved Person, precious to God and therefore precious to me. I am praying that no problem or pain will come between you and your love for God. *You can stand* against all trials, including sickness and disaster, in complete faith in the One you love. You're not to be discouraged. The gifts of the Spirit are yours because you are free to be used by God. You do not deny yourself the good gifts of God. You take them willingly and openly because you love Him. Nothing can conquer you, not even death. All that you touch is turned to love. The ultimate love experience is yours.

CHRISTIAN HERALD ASSOCIATION AND ITS MINISTRIES

CHRISTIAN HERALD ASSOCIATION, founded in 1878, publishes The Christian Herald Magazine, one of the leading interdenominational religious monthlies in America. Through its wide circulation, it brings inspiring articles and the latest news of religious developments to many families. From the magazine's pages came the initiative for CHRISTIAN HERALD CHILDREN'S HOME and THE BOWERY MISSION, two individually supported not-for-profit corporations.

CHRISTIAN HERALD CHILDREN'S HOME, established in 1894, is the name for a unique and dynamic ministry to disadvantaged children, offering hope and opportunities which would not otherwise be available for reasons of poverty and neglect. The goal is to develop each child's potential and to demonstrate Christian compassion and understanding to children in need.

Mont Lawn is a permanent camp located in Bushkill, Pennsylvania. It is the focal point of a ministry which provides a healthful "vacation with a purpose" to children who without it would be confined to the streets of the city. Up to 1000 children between the ages of 7 and 11 come to Mont Lawn each year.

Christian Herald Children's Home maintains year-round contact with children by means of an *In-City Youth Ministry*. Central to its philosophy is the belief that only through sustained relationships and demonstrated concern can individual lives be truly enriched. Special emphasis is on individual guidance, spiritual and family counseling and tutoring. This follow-up ministry to inner-city children culminates for many in financial assistance toward higher education and career counseling.

THE BOWERY MISSION, located at 227 Bowery, New York City, has since 1879 been reaching out to the lost men on the Bowery, offering them what could be their last chance to rebuild their lives. Every man is fed, clothed and ministered to. Countless numbers have entered the 90-day residential rehabilitation program at the Bowery Mission. A concentrated ministry of counseling, medical care, nutrition therapy, Bible study and Gospel services awakens a man to spiritual renewal within himself.

These ministries are supported solely by the voluntary contributions of individuals and by legacies and bequests. Contributions are tax deductible. Checks should be made out either to CHRISTIAN HERALD CHILDREN'S HOME or to THE BOWERY MISSION.

Administrative Office: 40 Overlook Drive, Chappaqua, New York 10514
Telephone: (914) 769-9000